The Food Contrarian
Quotes for People Recovering from
or Dealing with Eating Issues

Carl "Tuchy" Palmieri

*Dedication: This collection of quotes, adages, sayings, and points to ponder is a result of years of involvement and guidance from many people familiar with the 12-step program of Alcoholics Anonymous and offshoots such as **OVEREATERS ANONYMOUS**. I want to thank the many people in my life who introduced me to recovery programs.*

To M. Scott Peck, who advised all attendees at one of his workshops to find an excuse to get into any 12-step program. To my dear friend John Moser, who labored over theses writings to insure their accuracy and applicability; to Dale Kesten, my friend who helped me so much to find answers. And to my wife, Susan Palmieri, who has supported me through thick and thin in my pursuit of self-discovery. And finally to our wonderful children; Kathleen, Phil, Amy, John, and Stephen.

This book is also dedicated to all the people in all recovery programs, especially to the sponsors, who carry the message. Let us all remember those wonderful people whose bottom took them from this earth too soon.

In loving memory of my brother, Vincent Palmieri

INTRODUCTION

PLEASE NOTE: THESE WRITINGS ARE NOT APPROVED BY O.A. OR ANY OTHER PROGRAM.

In my 22 years of working 12-step programs I have found that the eating disorders dwarfed other addictions. I am grateful that I was able to pass through other addictions-- smoking, coffee, alcohol-- to find the true addiction for me. The most dangerous disease to have is the one that you do not know you have. This is most true with food, as it manifests in so many ways-- overeating, under-eating (anorexia), bulimia, and countless combinations.

The intention is that this collection of sayings, quotes, and thoughts brings help to recovering people. From a simple laugh to helpful insights, and in the spirit of taking what works and leaving the rest, you are encouraged to do so. Many have found that when read on a daily basis, they gain insight, confidence and courage to overcome their specific problem(s).

QUOTATIONS ABOUT BOOKS AND READING

A good book on your shelf is a friend that turns its back on you and remains a friend.

-Author Unknown

Anyone who says they have only one life to live must not know how to read a book.

-Author Unknown

Let books be your dining table,
And you shall be full of delights
Let them be your mattress
And you shall sleep restful nights.

-Author Unknown

A book is like a garden carried in the pocket.

-Chinese proverb

A dirty book is rarely dusty.

-Author Unknown

COMPULSIVE EATER

1) For the compulsive overeater putting your foot in your mouth is bad; putting food in is worse.

2) The dilemma is that we often try to feed the mind with food for the body.

3) No amount of money and no amount of food can satisfy hunger that starts in the mind.

4) The road to obesity is paved with compulsive bites and roofed with empty calories.

5) Mind/body food.

6) The actual resisting of one's persistence strengthens the disease rather than diminishing it.

7) Food fix. It's any food you eat outside the food plan that you have.

8) Best food trade-off: trading your food for spiritual and emotional food.

9) Eating a balanced meal is a start, eating a healthy balanced meal is progress, eating a healthy balanced meal with the proper portions is success.

10) It is not only what you eat that counts; it is also what you don't eat.

11) Be good to yourself; the food you eat today is carried by your body tomorrow.

12) Being fed up is what is needed to break the eating cycle.

13) It is better to eat the right food in the wrong amount than the wrong food in the right amount.

14) The overeater eventually learns that more is not better.

15) For the anorexic, more is better.

16) It appears that the shortest distance is from the table to my stomach.

17) The truth is I have had many reasons for gaining weight, and many reasons for losing weight.

"Then, without realizing it, you try to improve yourself at the start of each new day; of course, you achieve quite a lot in the course of time. Anyone can do this; it costs nothing and is certainly very helpful. Whoever doesn't know it must learn and find by experience that a quiet conscience makes one strong."

-Anne Frank

COMPULSIVE EATER-CONTINUED

18) The diet progression: the seesaw, the yo-yo, and finally the boomerang diet.

19) Spiritual and emotional anorexia leads to compulsive eating.

20) The solution to eating disorders may be corrected with vision. The compulsive overeater sees things smaller than they are and the anorexic sees things bigger than they are.

21) Immaculate ingestion- consumption without the normal consequences.

22) Overeating is like pouring water over the embers of the spiritual flame.

23) The bitter taste of relapse overpowers the food that is eaten compulsively.

24) There are none so blind as a compulsive eater who cannot see.

25) When an overeater is compulsively eating he has fear and he gets frozen in his tracks, when the overeater has a food plan he has the courage to stand on high ground.

26) Compulsive overeater: acting like a banana.

27) Anorexic- string bean.

28) Failure to have a food plan is planning to fail.

29) Bulimic… any food will do.

30) The bread of life for the overeater: a giant sub for a snack.

31) The first apple kept God away, the second apple kept the doctor away, the third apple started the overeater down the path of pain and suffering.

32) Compulsive eating: letting the past disrupt the present so much so that the future is shortened.

33) A sweet tooth often produces a bitter result.

34) Eat one day's food one day at a time.

"Few will have the greatness to bend history itself; but each of us can work to change a small portion of events, and in the total of all those acts will be written the history of this generation."

-Robert F. Kennedy

COMPULSIVE EATER-CONTINUED

35) Black magic-- when one gains weight just by looking at food.

36) The question is not whether or not you like to eat. The question is whether or not you like to overeat.

37) Freedom comes when you with God are free from compulsive eating.

38) Just taking the food away from the compulsive eater does no better than cutting off one's hand to stop one from eating.

39) Compulsive eating... food for the body when the mind and spirit are hungry.

40) For the overeater adding an inch is a cinch.

41) For the anorexic losing an inch is a cinch.

42) The compulsive eater never lets logic interfere with their eating.

APPETIZER: PHYSICAL FOOD

SALAD: EMOTIONAL FOOD

MAIN COURSE: SPIRITUAL FOOD

DESSERT: GOD

FOOD

1) The problem came when we added butter to the bread of life.

2) The overweight problem came when we added butter to the bread of life. –John Moser

3) Only man can turn the bread of life into the bread of death.

4) Wear it or waste it. –Susie Palmieri

5) We were all born with hunger that cannot be satisfied with food ALONE.

6) Are you eating your food or is your food eating you?

7) When practical, it is God's will that we give food away to the poor; when it's not, God's will is that we throw it away rather than eating excess food.

8) Taking in some spiritual food curbs your appetite.

9) Food is either your fuel or your shelter.

10) Contrary to popular opinion you can eventually gain weight by just thinking about food; do it often enough and long enough, and the thoughts will drive you to action.

11) Enough food is fuel; too much food is shelter.

12) I was told to eat, drink, and be merry. I did the first two, but the third eluded me, so I kept trying. I eventually found that no matter how much I ate or drank I did not really get merry.

13) The pounds are in the pudding.

14) Some food is bitter to the very last bite.

15) Food fight-- when the food throws you and you lose.

16) Eating right tips the scales in your favor.

17) Cinnamon today keeps cholesterol at bay.

18) No matter how much I ate or drank I was unable to get merry.

"The relationship between commitment and doubt is by no means an antagonistic one. Commitment is healthiest when it is not without doubt but in spite of doubt."

-Rollo May

FOOD-CONTINUED

19) With food it is especially important to take what works and leave the rest.

20) A balanced diet includes food for your spirit, mind, and body.

21) A balanced diet includes spiritual, emotional, and physical food.

22) A balanced diet requires food from the primary food groups: spiritual food group, emotional food group, and the physical food group.

23) Feed your emotions rather than eat over them.

24) What is needed in your diet is more food for thought.

25) The truth is prepared food and a lie is convenient food.

26) Fast food takes you where you do not want to go too soon.

27) Comfort food will eventually make you very uncomfortable.

28) When you feed others you are fed.

29) PROGRAM SLOGAN: keep it simple (no fixings).

30) Check to see if after the first helping that the food is really helping.

31) Love is a food that has no calories.

32) "Poor me" is junk food for the mind.

33) Crumbs are a feast to an anorexic.

34) A good food plan includes food for the mind, body, and spirit.

35) A well-balanced meal includes the proper nutrients for the mind, body, and soul.

36) Alcohol is nothing but food that has been altered for consumption.

37) Alcohol is but good food that went bad.

38) The food of the program will never harm you.

39) When you get bored with conventional fruit try fruit of the sea.

"The greatest danger for most of us is not that our aim is too high and we miss it, but that it is too low and we reach it."

-Michelangelo

FOOD-CONTINUED

40) The bitterness of broccoli Rabe is to remind one that eating bitter food can be the sweetest thing to do.

41) Failing to have a food plan is planning to fail.

42) Man cannot live by bread alone did not mean that man should take the example of the pig and eat everything. It meant for us to ingest food for the mind and the spirit, to sustain life.

43) Not all food is created equal.

44) Contrary to some people's belief, food does not move.

45) Food fight--when the food wins.

46) Food, like money, is a good servant but a poor master.

47) Often one can have sweet results from eating bitter food.

48) It is a mystery with food, "How can little things make us so big?"

49) Comfort food eventually makes one uncomfortable.

"It is unwise to be too sure of one's own wisdom. It is healthy to be reminded that the strongest might weaken and the wisest might err."

-Mohandas K. Gandhi

HEALTH

1) Your best wealth is your health.

2) Eating truffles is not trifle.

3) Not all food is fuel.

4) Sometimes the best food you can give someone that is poor is food that will enable him to eat for life.

5) Medical science has advanced so far that today you can get a prescription of medication for your medication.

6) Diet- remove the "T" from "diet" and what do you have?

7) Wear it or waste it. –Susie Palmieri

8) You are what you eat.

9) Detox your spiritual, emotional, and physical being.

10) Resentment, envy, and hatred are toxins to the spirit, mind, and body.

11) Are those fixings really fixing?

12) What are your spiritual and emotional toxins?

13) One of the shortest ways to a man's heart attack is through his stomach.

14) Love is a food that feeds all and includes all the necessary ingredients to keep one healthy.

15) Take what works and leave the rest (stay away from your trigger food).

16) Easy does it (go light on the portions).

17) Zero calorie food: love, service, tolerance, kindness, forgiveness, and acceptance.

18) Food not recommended by the O/A program: anger, hate, resentment, lust, self-centeredness, pride.

19) Some natural ingredients produce unnatural results.

"In his later years Pablo Picasso was not allowed to roam an art gallery unattended, for he had previously been discovered in the act of trying to improve on one of his old masterpieces."

-*Unknown*

HEALTH-CONTINUED

20) Too many helpings produce many sicknesses.

21) Fill your head with the right food and your body will get all the nourishment it needs.

22) Anorexic: a contrarian glutton. –John Moser

23) Cleanse your emotional palate with quiet time.

24) A gluttonous body leads to a gluttonous mind.

25) The reason one man's meat is another man's poison is that we are all unique and general solutions often are dangerous.

26) Even the bread of life can kill you if taken to excess.

27) Even in the land of milk and honey there are foods that when taken to excess will kill.

28) The loaves and fishes are to be shared and when shared the body is well; when hoarded the body gets sick.

29) For some people real growth comes not from eating more but from eating less.

30) Hitting your TOP is like depression… it is the first step towards feeling better.

31) Hitting your TOP is the first step towards getting better.

32) It makes little difference if the toxins are ingested through the body or the mind; the result is the same illness.

33) Removing the toxins from the spirit and the mind enables the body to do likewise.

34) Just as it does no good to fuel up a car and just leave it idling, it does no good to eat heartily and be a couch potato.

35) Acquiring a taste for life may be one of your best ways to ensure what you eat does not eat you.

36) Fertilize your mind with organic thoughts.

"We know what we are, but know not what we may be."

-*William Shakespeare*

HEALTH-CONTINUED

37) You know you have a problem when you have eaten a hearty meal, your tummy is full and yet you continue to eat.

38) A sweet tooth, left unchecked, produces a bitter result.

39) There is no shortage of programs that offer snake oil magic for your eating problem.

40) For some people their wait problem causes their weight problem.

41) An ounce of determination yields an ounce of result.

42) What one does today often has as much impact on health as what one eats today.

43) Diets do not work because they are temporary in nature.

44) Some diets work for part of the time, and some diets the other part of the time, but no diet works for all time.

45) If the goal of a diet is to lose weight then any diet will do.

46) The oldest diet in the world is still the diet that works the fastest… the starvation diet.

47) The food we eat today will either bring us health or sickness.

48) Eat well today so that you can live tomorrow and eat well again.

49) Real joy: eating healthy food in a healthy way.

50) It's not the stone in the soup that one needs to be concerned about.

51) Laughter is indeed the best medicine.

52) Enjoy the banquet food for the mind, body, and soul.

"Don't waste life in doubts and fears; spend yourself on the work before you, well assured that the right performance of this hour's duties will be the best preparation for the hours and ages that will follow it."

-Ralph Waldo Emerson

EATING

1) Taking two can lead to seeing the doctor in the morning.

2) The OA cookbook is filled with heart-healthy recipes.

3) Feed your spirit; feed your mind.

4) Take your spiritual vitamins and your emotional minerals.

5) Real soul food cannot be ingested through the mouth (stomach).

6) Eat like a horse and have oats.

7) Do not try to eat like a bird as the typical bird consumes two to three times his weight each day.

8) Vegetarians have good taste.

9) One bite at a time.

10) Let (the food) go and let God.

11) The real question to ask is that helping, helping?

12) Just because the first serving serves you does not mean that the additional ones do the same, on the contrary, many will say they do not serve at all.

13) Feeding your spiritual body settles your physical stomach.

14) The program teaches you to eat to live rather than living to eat.

15) Harvest time: setting aside for a later time the food you need to nourish yourself.

16) Weighing and measuring the meal eliminates the need to weigh and measure after the meal.

17) Good food is good, and good food may or may not taste good.

18) Some of us take too much of a good thing and that makes it bad.

19) Alcohol: a modern-day version of the fruit from the tree of knowledge of good and evil.

20) The first apple kept God away; the next apple keeps the doctor away.

"Change is the law of life. And those who look only to the past or present are certain to miss the future."

-John F. Kennedy

EATING-CONTINUED

21) Failing to have a food plan is planning to fail.

22) The best way to look at your food is to view it as a double-edged sword. On one edge it does what it is supposed to do and on the other it cuts and can kill.

23) When your need for food goes beyond the food you need, then you need the help of God to reduce your need.

24) Binge is what happens to you as it relates to food once you pass the point of having a normal meal.

25) Beware, that bottomless pit may actually grow into the fruit of your stomach.

26) The best starvation diet is the one that starves the compulsive eating.

27) Many of us would do well to replace the scale we stand on with the scale we measure with.

28) The past meals have passed; the future meals may not come. Today's meal, however, is the one that determines your life.

29) You can eat an elephant if you cut it up in enough small pieces.

30) Beware of small pieces.

31) When one sours on sweets, one is in a very sweet place.

32) Often it's the sweet little morsels that produce the bitter result of obesity.

"The dogmas of the quiet past are inadequate to the stormy present. The occasion is piled high with difficulty, and we must rise with the occasion. As our case is new, so we must think anew and act anew."

-*Abraham Lincoln*

SPIRITUAL

1) A good sermon is to the soul what a good meal is to the body.

2) God… my spiritual sponsor.

3) It does not matter what my spiritual food plan consists of; what matters is that I have a plan.

4) It is very difficult to overeat on spiritual food.

5) Real comfort food comforts the body, mind, and spirit.

6) When you ingest spiritual food you never eat alone.

7) Not all food is intended to be ingested through the mouth.

8) Opening your mouth prevents some food from entering the body.

9) We learn that shutting the mouth opens the way to feed your spiritual being.

10) The program is where the emotional meets the physical and gets spiritual.

11) Take care of your spiritual health and your physical health will improve.

12) Real health food feeds more than the body.

13) Health food-- prayer, meditation, love, kindness, service, etc.

14) Spiritual health food store-- church, synagogue, meeting hall.

15) Spiritual health food store-- O/A program.

16) Recovery from compulsive eating is found in your local spiritual health food store.

17) One cannot eat enough food to quell spiritual and emotional hunger.

18) The new food pyramid suggests having five to nine servings of spiritual food to have a balanced day.

19) If you find yourself in a place where you just cannot get to a normal weight, know that you cannot get you there, and that another can.

"Let us rise up and be thankful, for if we didn't learn a lot today, at least we learned a little, and if we didn't learn a little, at least we didn't get sick, and if we got sick, at least we didn't die; so, let us all be thankful."

-Buddha

SPIRITUAL-CONTINUED

20) God grant me the wisdom to know that You are there for me, the courage to ask for Your help, and the serenity to know that if I keep working Your help will come.

21) Doctor Palmieri states that there is no limit on the amount of spiritual food you can eat; you are free to eat as much as you like.

22) An ounce of determination with the help of God weighs more than a ton on your own.

23) Satisfaction in food comes from soul satisfaction.

24) Many foods defy the law of gravity.

25) A program paradox: some of us need inflation of the spirit, before deflation (inflation) of the body occurs.

26) An aching heart or a tortured soul are often mistaken for an empty stomach.

27) The most nourishing buffet is one that feeds the spirit.

28) The real bread of life comes not from the grain, but from the spirit.

BINGE:

Blind

Indulgence

Notwithstanding

Good

Eating

DISEASE

1) The disease of compulsive eating is like the disease of cancer; if left unchecked they will take your life.

2) Bulimia: two wrongs to make right.

3) Bulimia: an irrational act attempting to correct an irrational act.

4) Waste it or wear it. –Susie Palmieri

5) Glutton: one who knows the answer and chooses to ignore it.

6) You cannot satisfy your hunger with just physical food.

7) Insanity-- weighing and measuring after the meal.

8) Before the program I weighed and measured.

9) The bread of life for the anorexic-- wheat thins once per day.

10) The jaws of death lose their strength by staying closed more often.

11) As it is not that money is evil, but that the love of money is evil, so it is with food it is not the food that is dangerous it's the love of food that is evil.

12) Some of God's food has been improved by man and some food has been poisoned by the hands of man.

13) Before you take that first bite, make sure the other man's meat is not your poison.

14) The compulsive bite is the descendent of the apple.

15) The disease-- you either take care of it or it will take care of you.

16) Purge: an attempt to correct a mistake with another mistake.

17) It is not so much the "what" of eating that gets you in trouble, as it is the "why" of eating.

18) It is impossible to measure the bitterness that can come from a sweet tooth.

"As we express our gratitude, we must never forget that the highest appreciation is not to utter words, but to live by them."

-*John F. Kennedy*

DISEASE-CONTINUED

19) Waiting for your weight to normalize is like waiting for your ship to come in.

20) Relapse-- when your disease is in recovery.

21) It's the addiction that gets you by the ounce.

22) The problem is when we attempt to solve all our hunger with food.

23) Some diets work for the rest of people's lives, the only problem is that the rest of their lives are very short.

24) Binge: when enough is not enough.

25) All one needs to do is look at the food label of ingredients to know that the devil is in the details.

26) Overfeeding anything will bring it death or disease.

27) Recount the calories.

28) Some people work, some people follow, and still others just come along for the ride.

29) For the overeater too much is too little.

"Gratitude is not only the greatest of virtues, but the parent of all the others."

-Cicero

DISEASE-CONTINUED

30) For the anorexic too little is too much.

31) When young some of us were underfed, some were overfed, and yet others were misfed.

32) For some a piece of cake does not mean easy but the opposite, as they must work hard to undo the effect of taking the piece of cake.

33) World's number one diet: the yo-yo diet.

34) A spiritual buffet feeds the soul.

35) Question: Whom is that next serving serving?

36) The problem may be that I am denying my denial.

37) DIET: Doing Insane Eating Temporary.

38) No matter how you slice it, too much is too much and too little is too little.

"It doesn't work to leap a twenty-foot chasm in two ten-foot jumps."

   -American proverb

BIG BOOK/ GOOD BOOK QUOTES

1) One must be careful that they do not get so hot that they melt their clay feet and lose their footing.

2) Be glad you are off the wall; it gives one freedom to move.

3) A slip is when you stop doing the same thing over and over and expecting the same result.

4) When you are in the rooms and not doing the steps you are only safe if you can walk on dangerous waters.

5) The compulsive eater proved the proverb that watch out for your friends and love your enemies. Their friend food became their enemy and their enemies became their friends.

6) I never knew an insane person who did not know.

7) The progress of prayer—pray to, pray for, pray with.

8) We are told ask and you shall receive, so if you have not received you may not have asked enough.

9) How politicians see the 12 steps: the conservative sees God, the liberal has a higher power, the independent sees a universal force, and the green party sees love and tolerance.

10) You alone have no power; you and the group high power, God higher power, you and God the highest power for you.

One night a man had a dream. He dreamed he was walking along the beach with the Lord. Across the sky flashed scenes from his life. For each scene he noticed two sets of footprints in the sand: One belonged to him and the other to the Lord.

When the last scene of his life flashed before him, he looked back at the footprints in the sand. He noticed many times along the path of his life there was only one set of footprints. He also noticed that it happened at the very lowest and saddest times in his life.

This really bothered him and he questioned the Lord about it. Lord, You said that once I decided to follow You, You'd walk with me all the way. But I have noticed that during the most troublesome times in my life there is only one set of footprints. I don't understand why when I needed You most You would leave me. The Lord replied, "My precious, precious child, I love you and I would never leave you during your times of trial and suffering. When you see one set of footprints, it was then that I carried you."

-Author Unknown

BIG BOOK/GOOD BOOK QUOTES-CONTINUED

11) Contrarian promises: you will feel good about shameful acts, you will embrace your character defects, and you will know real insanity.

12) The disease of alcoholism is like the disease of cancer; if left unchecked they will take your life.

13) When you follow more than one path you are never sure which one is right.

14) It makes no difference who inspires you, friend or foe; it just matters that you are inspired.

15) The only time some people go through the doors of a church is to attend a 12-step meeting.

16) Hazelden books—the apocrypha of the 12 steps.

17) Just because you think good does not mean you are a good thinker.

18) Strange, Bill and Dr. Bob did not recover by reading the big book.

19) Jesus did not read the Bible.

20) When you stop doing the steps you are actually taking a step backwards.

AA SLOGANS

It works… it really does! (Page 88, line 8 in the big book)

More will be revealed.

It's in the book.

When all else fails, follow directions.

Respect the anonymity of others.

Principles before personalities.

When we surrender to our higher power, the journey begins.

Fear stands for Frustration, Ego, Anxiety, and Resentment.

The 12 steps tell us how it works; the 12 traditions tell us why it works.

When man listens, God speaks; when man obeys, God works.

Your big book is your sponsor too.

BIG BOOK/GOOD BOOK QUOTES CONTINUED

21) It is strange but you actually slip when you stop rather than when you are taking steps.

22) It is the only place where you can slip when you stop.

23) The big book: one of the books that spreads the good news.

24) The real old-timers: the prophets of the big book.

25) The trinity of the 12 steps: spiritual, emotional, and physical.

26) 12 steps: the other trinity.

27) The big book—the drinking man's bible; the compulsive eater's gospel.

28) At first it loosens the tongue, then it twists it, and finally it quiets the tongue.

29) With recovery you are either recovering or you are not.

30) Beware of the Pharisees of the program.

31) Christ—the original protestant.

As children bring their broken toys,

With tears for us to mend,

I brought my broken dreams to God,

Because he is my friend.

But then instead of leaving Him

In peace to work alone,

I hung around and tried to help,

With ways that were my own.

At last, I snatched them back again

And cried, "How can you be so slow?"

"My child," He said, "What could I do?

You never did let go."

-Author unknown

BIG BOOK/GOOD BOOK QUOTES CONTINUED

32) You must leave the convex and concave mirrors in your life for the true mirrors in the fellowship.

33) The problem may not be that you are out of your mind but rather in your mind.

34) A.A. proves that history repeats itself.

35) Question: Whom did Bill and Dr. Bob follow?

36) It's the miracle of turning from wine to water.

37) The food of the program will never harm you.

38) The fellowship—brotherly love healing hearts.

39) The medicine prescribed by the program brings you relief from your disease. It is not for everyone. Consult with your sponsor to see if the 12 steps are for you. The side effects are peace, joy, love, serenity, happiness, and a conscious contact with God. Do not take this medicine if you suffer from the ability to be honest or if you are unwilling to be willing.

40) The Bible proves that the message of the written word changes.

41) The A.A. big book is a program guide based upon principles similar to the biblical teachings.

42) The A.A. big book is a program based upon ancient and universal principles.

43) The most nourishing and healthy recipes can be found in the good book, and the big book.

44) The Bible asks us to fast from food, not have fast food.

"Nothing worth doing is completed in our lifetime; therefore, we are saved by hope.

Nothing true or beautiful or good makes complete sense in any immediate context of history; therefore, we are saved by faith.

Nothing we do, however virtuous, can be accomplished alone. Therefore, we are saved by love.

No virtuous act is quite as virtuous from the standpoint of our friend or foe as from our own; therefore, we are saved by the final form of love, which is forgiveness."

-Reinhold Niebuhr

BIG BOOK/GOOD BOOK QUOTES CONTINUED

45) All food can be blessed but not all food is blessed.

46) In the Lord's Prayer we pray that His will be done, then we ask, "give us this day our daily bread."

47) The banquet you were promised is the food for the mind and soul.

48) The prophets of the program: Moses, Solomon.

49) Sugar is but a modern-day version of the forbidden fruit.

50) Sugar: A descendant of the apple.

51) Self-help health book: the Bible.

52) Self-help health book: The big book.

53) To recover throw away all the self-help books and turn to the God-help books: Bible, Old Testament, Koran, big book, etc.

54) Lent: 40 days of just for today.

55) Lent says I can give up for 40 days what I cannot give up forever.

56) Forgiveness gets rid of those that are renting space in your head.

57) All achievements great or small start with the same decision... I can do all things through you God, who strengthens me.

HUMILITY

Humility is the recognition of the allness of God
And the nothingness of self.

It is the lowly root that stiffens the great oak
Against storms of the centuries.

It is the father of confidence, the mother of joy,
The brother of courage, the sister of kindness.

It walks with wisdom,
Talks with truth,
And dwells with love.

True humility is not a garment, but a trait of character.

It never intrudes, often has to be discovered, it is never boisterous nor
self-assertive.

But if it is mistaken for weakness there is apt to be a rude awakening,
for the strength of humility lies in its impersonal selflessness, a
fundamental element of power.

It adds power to authority, credence to reason, and reverence to
spirituality.

THE BIG BOOK

1) The big book is like the good book in many ways... neither should be taken literally.

2) The problem with the big book comes when you don't take it literally.

3) The big book is actually on the small side, as far as books go.

4) For ME reading the big book is good; and reading it with the good book is better.

5) A dishonest mistake—a lie.

AA SLOGANS

Easy does it.

Live and let live.

One day at a time.

Let go and let God.

Expect miracles.

Keep coming back… it works if you work it.

Keep an open mind.

Pass it on.

90 meetings in 90 days… 90/90.

Use the 24-hour plan.

Call your sponsor before, not after, you take the first compulsive bite.

Help is only a phone call away.

Keep coming back… kcb.

THE PROGRAM

1)   It's where you discover you have not asked God enough.

2)   It turns flaming idiots into balls of fire that go around lighting everyone's candle.

3)   It's where people get religion.

4)   For some people the program is their religion of choice.

5)   One of the purposes of the program is to examine insanity.

6)   Some call it magic.

7)   The program is about changing your thinking from over thinking to rethinking.

8)   Program instruments: a drum, a horn, and a fiddle.

9)   Program utensils: a can opener, spatula, tongs, and a nutcracker.

10)   A program that takes a person out of his mind and out of the world.

11)   Program tools: a hammer, an air compressor, a drill, a broom, and a jackhammer.

1. You will receive a body.
You may like it or hate it, but it will be yours for the entire period this time around.

2. You will learn lessons.
You are enrolled in a full-time, informal school called "life." Each day in this school you will have the opportunity to learn lessons. You may like the lessons or think them irrelevant and stupid.

3. There are no mistakes, only lessons.
Growth is a process of trial and error, experimentation. The "failed" experiments are as much a part of the process as the experiment that "works."

4. A lesson is repeated until it is learned.
A lesson will be presented to you in various forms until you have learned it. Then you can go on to the next lesson.

5. Learning lessons does not end.
There is no part of life that does not contain its lessons. If you are alive, there are lessons to be learned.

6. "There" is no better than "here."
When your "there" has become a "here," you will simply obtain another "there" that, again, looks better than "here."

7. Others are merely mirrors of you.
You cannot love or hate something about another person unless it reflects to you something you love or hate about yourself.

8. What you make of your life is up to you.
You have all the tools and resources you need; what you do with them is up to you. The choice is yours.

9. The answers lie inside you.
The answers to life's questions lie inside you. All you need to do is look, listen, and trust.

-Author unknown

PONDERING THE STEPS

1) Some people do the steps by sidestepping.

2) Some people take such small steps that they never get their feet high enough to the ground.

3) Skipping steps is one of the surest ways to slip.

4) Even a normal person will slip if he tries to skip steps.

5) Going back one step can be a giant step forward.

6) If you turn around before you take a step, you will never go backwards.

7) Sidestepping is the way we get stuck.

8) When you find that you are stuck on a step, check to see if you are sidestepping.

9) Side-stepping does not move you forward.

10) If your steps are not built on the foundation of God, then you will eventually crumble.

11) For me the 12 steps are about uncovering your tracks and walking in the footsteps of God.

12) The steps go both ways.

Our Father, who art in Heaven

Hallowed be thy name.

Thy Kingdom come, Thy will be done,

On Earth as it is in Heaven.

Give us this day our daily bread and forgive us our trespasses

As we forgive those who trespass against us.

And lead us not into temptation

But deliver us from evil

For Thine is the Kingdom, the Power, and the Glory forever.

Amen.

PONDERING THE STEPS-CONTINUED

13) Members need the steps to pick them up and others need the steps to take them down.

14) Not doing the steps is like having a toothache and not doing anything about it. Sooner or later the ache will take you down, as will any disease.

15) Some people want the steps to do them.

16) Some people want the steps to take the action. (John Moser)

17) To take the recovery path you must take steps.

18) Desire earns you a seat in the rooms; taking the steps keeps placing you there.

19) You are finished once you finish with the steps.

20) Where the journey begins after the final step.

21) The least valid statement in the program: "I have finished the steps."

22) Some people are willing to go to any steps rather than go to all lengths.

23) Some people are willing to go to different steps rather than go to any length.

12 SIGNS OF A SPIRITUAL AWAKENING

1. An increased tendency to let things happen rather than make them happen.

2. Frequent attacks of smiling.

3. Feelings of being connected with others and nature.

4. Frequent overwhelming episodes of appreciation.

5. A tendency to think and act spontaneously rather than from fears based on past experience.

6. An unmistakable ability to enjoy each moment.

7. A loss of ability to worry.

8. A loss of interest in conflict.

9. A loss of interest in interpreting the actions of others.

10. A loss of interest in judging others.

11. A loss of interest in judging self.

12. Gaining the ability to love without expecting anything in return.

-Source unknown

GENERAL PONDERING

1) An honest lie—one you believe in.

2) Make sure the diamond in the rough is not just an ordinary piece of coal.

3) A piece of coal is but a diamond in the rough.

4) You really do not have to be one to know one.

5) A dishonest mistake—a lie.

6) Too many of us corrected our honest mistakes with dishonest ones.

7) I never knew an insane person who did not know.

8) How strange; as you get stronger you pick up less, if at all.

9) Hitting your bottom is like depression—it is the first step towards feeling better.

10) Hitting your bottom is the first step towards getting better.

11) Bottoms up is one of the surest ways to hit your bottom.

12) A high bottom is not on one's body.

13) Asking a roach to deroach himself is like asking a tiger to remove his stripes.

14) A point to ponder—is accepting the things you cannot change an act of serenity, or an act of sanity?

15) Not being normal can be a very good thing.

"How would it be if just for today we thought less about contests and rivalries, profits and politics, winners and sinners and more about helping and giving, mending and blending, reaching out and pitching in? How would it be?"

-Anonymous

GENERAL PONDERING-CONTINUED

16) Do not ask if you are normal or not, but ask what side of normal you are.

17) The only difference between sanity and insanity is the time we are acting in each.

18) A question: If a sane person performed an insane act is he really insane? Conversely, if an insane person did a sane act, is he sane?

19) An insane act can make a sane person insane, and yet a sane act by an insane person does not make him sane.

20) If you ask enough people, all apples are bad.

21) I am sorry for those of us who are normal as they are not free.

22) It is possible to get good fruit from a bad tree.

23) Going to any length includes all length.

24) Not all mirrors reflect back at you.

25) The mirror you are using may not reflect back properly.

26) A big person is not very big at all.

27) If you are going to shoot the messenger at least wait until the message has been delivered.

28) Disorganization is a key to success.

29) The signs on the road you travel depend upon the direction you are traveling.

30) Being grateful for being able to have your round peg in a square hole.

BE THANKFUL

Be thankful that you don't already have everything you desire.
If you did, what would there be to look forward to?

Be thankful when you don't know something.
For it gives you the opportunity to learn.

Be thankful for the difficult times.
During those times you grow.

Be thankful for your limitations.
Because they give you opportunities for improvements.

Be thankful for each new challenge.
Because it will build your strength and character.

Be thankful for your mistakes.
They will teach you valuable lessons.

Be thankful when you're tired and weary.

A life of rich fulfillment comes to those
Who are also thankful for the setbacks.

Gratitude can turn a negative into a positive.
Find a way to be thankful for your troubles
And they can become your blessings.

GENERAL PONDERING-CONTINUED

31) What a sad world it would be if everything fit perfectly and worked perfectly.

32) The disease is like a cockroach; you can never eliminate it, you can only control it with a de-roaching process.

33) I hit my bottom in '87 and hit my top in '91.

34) I prefer being off the wall than being a still life on the wall.

35) If you are not off the wall then you are not moving and have a still life.

36) Does a fly on the wall really care what you are saying or are doing?

37) The messenger can change the meaning of the words without changing the words.

38) Do not try to change the messenger rather than changing the words.

39) Changing the messenger does not change the message.

40) I know you know it all, but I'm not sure you know that all you know is not all there is to know.

41) It is a verbal book club that listens to the same stories over and over again.

42) It is a program of reciprocal promises.

43) The question is, do you see it as a spiritual program of recovery, or is it a program of spiritual recovery?

44) Abstinence allows one to begin their emotional and spiritual recovery.

45) Making a decision is a good start; acting on it is success.

Holding your head high, and being the best you know you can be when life seems to fall apart at your feet, facing each difficulty with the confidence that time will bring you better tomorrows, and never giving up, means confidence.

-Author unknown

GENERAL PONDERING-CONTINUED

46) Taking what is said out of the rooms is a sin against the program.

47) An attitude of gratitude increases your altitude and enables you to soar above the turbulence of life.

48) When an overeater is eating compulsively he has fear and he gets frozen in his tracks; when the compulsive eater gets abstinent he has the courage to stand on high ground.

49) When a compulsive eater has fear he gets drowsy on the couch; when the compulsive eater has courage he stands on high ground.

50) It is important to grasp the point that he knows he's not all there; then he is able to grasp the will of God.

51) Just because you are moving, that does not mean you are taking the steps.

52) An INACTIVE compulsive eater—one who is active with the steps.

53) Making a decision in step three is a good start; acting on it is success.

54) One who has accepted his calling.

55) To give is more powerful than to receive.

56) Bill Wilson—an example of the power of giving over receiving.

57) The critical step is when a person takes to making amends.

58) A fellowship of believers who trust in God and believe they received a gift in order to give it away.

59) Let us not forget the real intent of a boomerang is to give you a second chance.

Meetings satisfy hunger for fellowship, and quench our thirst for friendship.

Service satisfies hunger for usefulness, and quenches the thirst for purpose.

Anonymity satisfies hunger for security and quenches the thirst for privacy.

Writing satisfies hunger for clarity, and quenches the thirst for recording.

Literature satisfies hunger for guidance and quenches the thirst for information.

Telephone satisfies hunger for a response to a call for help, and quenches the thirst for those hard-to-handle situations.

Food plan satisfies hunger for simplicity and quenches the thirst for freedom from obsession.

Sponsorship satisfies hunger for reciprocation and quenches the thirst for helping others.

GENERAL PONDERING-CONTINUED

60) Think less; do more.

61) Don't worry about losing weight; if you are like most people you will find it again.

62) Let go of anything that hurts you or others.

63) Many die never having satisfied their hunger.

64) For some, doing the footwork means tap dancing.

65) The letting go of resistance nullifies the persistence.

66) To get a different answer, ask a different question.

67) An ounce of determination now can save you pounds in the future.

68) For many the real problem is not in giving but in receiving.

69) If you hang in long enough, you eventually let go.

70) I owe my life to my enemy (my disease) so I love my enemy.

71) The problem started after I made a commitment to eat, drink, and be merry. That was the start of denial.

72) Going the extra mile… getting up, walking or driving to get your food fix.

73) No matter how thin you slice it, or how much you pound it, when it goes in, it will have the same result.

74) The best triangle is the complete food pyramid.

75) Weight control starts with being fed up. –John Moser

"Common-looking people are the best in the world: that is the reason the Lord makes so many of them."

-Abraham Lincoln

GENERAL PONDERING-CONTINUED

76) You are similar to an engine; you need the right fuel in the right combination.

77) Try eating your thoughts.

78) An herb a day keeps the doctor away.

79) The gift of choice can be your greatest gift or your greatest curse.

80) Software- your thoughts. Hardware- your body. To correct your body may require changing your software.

81) Our disease can be understood better when compared to a trainer of dangerous wild animals. When the trainer uses his tools and takes the right steps, the animal will do as he is told. If he stops using a tool or misses a step, he finds that the animal will turn on him. To be safe he must always be on guard.

82) I am on a see-food diet. I see food and I eat it.

83) If the truth is inconvenient some people will not go there.

84) The truth may be too inconvenient for him.

85) In relapse: being dishonest about one's dishonesty.

86) A rational liar: one in denial.

87) The platinum affirmation: I am roached up.

88) We don't ask you to surrender we merely ask you to acknowledge that you have surrendered to your disease already.

89) A polished lie: no artificial ingredients.

"The truth is that our finest moments are most likely to occur when we are feeling deeply uncomfortable, unhappy, or unfulfilled. For it is only in such moments, propelled by our discomfort, that we are likely to step out of our ruts and start searching for different ways or truer answers."

-M. Scott Peck

GENERAL PONDERING-CONTINUED

90) If it sounds too good to be true, and you want to hear it, it most likely is not true, if you do not want to hear it then you have a good chance that it is true.

91) Ignorance of the facts does not make them any less dangerous.

92) You cannot change anything you are not aware of.

93) To know and not do is to really not know.

94) At a feast one would do best to feast their eyes rather than their stomach.

95) Fasting is to the body what meditation is to the mind.

96) One of the few times in life when you get happier having less of what you like.

97) Inaccurate truth: an accurate statement that is meant to mislead.

98) It's the only program that you hit your bottom when you hit your top.

99) Most apples are bad.

100) If you ask enough people, all apples are bad.

101) It is possible to get good fruit from a bad tree.

102) The mirror you are using may not reflect back properly.

103) I hit my bottom in '87 and hit my top in '91.

104) It's actually not just what you eat it is also what eats you.

105) Often it is what is eating you that makes you indulge.

"To forget how to dig the earth and to tend the soil is to forget ourselves."

-Mohandas K. Gandhi

GENERAL PONDERING-CONTINUED

106) Your weight problem disappears when your wait problem disappears.

107) An agitated mind leads to an agitated body.

108) The sick soul disturbs the mind and the disturbed mind takes it out on the body.

109) A stomach ache is the body's way of telling you that what you put into it may have been wrong; the heartache is the mind's way of telling you it was fed something wrong.

110) What comes out of your mouth is more important than what goes into it, what comes from the heart is more important.

111) The bread of life for the normal person: a slice of multigrain with each meal.

112) Man can exist on bread alone, but he cannot live.

113) St. Peter was one of the many predecessors of the program.

114) The meaning of serenity per the serenity prayer—acceptance, courage, and wisdom.

115) The reason most self-help books eventually fail is that no man is an island.

116) It's not in the genes; it's in the grain. –John Moser

117) Fertilize the mind with organic thoughts.

118) The nourishment you get today started with the seeds you planted yesterday. Plant GOOD SEEDS for the body, mind, and spirit.

119) From my powerlessness comes power; and from my power comes powerlessness.

1) Faith instead of despair.

2) Courage instead of fear.

3) Hope instead of desperation.

4) Peace of mind instead of confusion.

5) Real friendship instead of loneliness.

6) Self-respect instead of self-contempt.

7) Self-confidence instead of helplessness.

8) A clean conscience instead of a sense of guilt.

9) The respect of others instead of their pity and contempt.

10) A clean pattern of living instead of a hopeless existence.

11) The love and understanding of our families instead of their doubts and fears.

12) The freedom of a happy life instead of the bondage of an eating obsession.

GENERAL PONDERING-CONTINUED

120) An educated consumer is the junk food industry's worst customer.

121) An uneducated consumer is the junk food industry's best customer.

122) Let not your love of food be so intense that it harms you.

123) For many men their hairline decreases as their waistline increases.

124) Before you eat something you like make sure that something likes you.

125) Most of us want the plum and do not want the pit, and yet it is the pit that will keep us eating plums.

126) From the manure of the mind, when fed by God, becomes the fertilizer that helps one grow into a peach of a man.

127) Waiting alone seldom solves your weight problem.

128) The problem is not so much the diet; the problem is what comes after the diet.

129) There are many people who are on diets their entire life, so from that viewpoint diets work.

130) Letting go allows acceptance and acceptance allows one to let go.

131) Often we get ease confused with simplicity.

132) When I admitted that I believed I could not handle my disease alone, the struggling and resisting stopped. This was my first incident of letting go.

133) Trade in your shovels for teaspoons.

Stuff That Makes You Feel Good

Think about each one for a while before going on to the next...

Falling in love.

Laughing so hard your face hurts.

A special glance.

Getting mail.

Taking a drive on a pretty road.

Hearing your favorite song on the radio.

Lying in bed listening to the rain outside.

Hot towels fresh out of the dryer.

Finding the sweater you want is on sale for half price.

A chocolate milk shake. (Or vanilla) (Or strawberry). (But not for most of us.)

A long-distance phone call.

A bubble bath.

Giggling.

A good conversation.

Finding $20 in your coat from last winter.

Running through sprinklers.

Laughing for no reason at all.

Friends.

Accidentally overhearing someone say something nice about you.

Watching the sunrise.

Your first kiss (either the very first or with a new partner).

Making new friends or spending time with old ones.

Playing with a puppy.

Sweet dreams.

THE 12 STEPS

1) Some people believe they can recover by sidestepping.

2) The 12 steps are straight and narrow; if you sidestep you will fall off the path.

3) Practicing the 12 steps is the best way to learn how to stay on the wagon.

4) There are two kinds of people in the 12-step program: those who step too, and those who step on others.

5) God is the railing in the 12-step program that you must hold onto for support as you do the steps.

6) Doing the steps requires you to pick up your feet.

7) Make sure the 12 steps you are taking are not taking you in circles.

8) A 12-stepper knows his mind is wasted.

9) A person doing the 12 steps will tell you that the mind is not a terrible thing to waste.

10) The 12 steps is akin to a recycling station; garbage in, clean material out.

11) In the context of the 12-step literature, bigger is better.

12) The big book—the 12-step bible.

13) The 12-step program teaches you that you do not need variety to have spice in your life.

14) The 12 steps is a process in which you are softened so that you can be remolded by the hands of God.

Step One satisfies our hunger for truth and awareness.

Step Two satisfies our hunger for hope.

Step Three satisfies our hunger for help.

Step Four satisfies our hunger for inner cleansing.

Step Five satisfies our hunger to disclose the undiscloseable.

Step Six satisfies our hunger for God's help.

Step Seven satisfies our hunger to let go and let God's forgiveness come.

Step Eight satisfies our hunger for awareness and willingness.

Step Nine satisfies our hunger for peace and forgiveness.

Step Ten satisfies our daily hunger.

Step Eleven satisfies our hunger to know our creator.

Step Twelve satisfies our hunger to help others.

THE 12 STEPS-CONTINUED

15) In the 12 steps we first listen to ourselves, then we listen to others, and finally we learn to listen to God.

16) Another 12-step definition of insanity: making changes over and over, expecting the results to stay the same.

17) Some people only need to take twelve steps on the pathway to God.

18) The 12-step program makes it ok to not be ok.

19) The 12 steps can be seen as the ultimate Protestant Movement.

20) The 12 steps are where you have insights about your insights.

21) Churches, synagogues, temples, and halls play a great role in the 12-step program. For some it's by going and others by not going.

22) A 12-stepper is a disciple of Bill and Doctor Bob.

23) A 12-stepper is an insane person who is no longer mad.

24) A 12-stepper is a reformed mad man.

25) On the recovery path there are 12 steps and three bridges—physical, emotional, and spiritual.

26) Pigeon—the unofficial bird of the 12 steps.

27) 12 steps—use universal laws to solve a specific problem.

28) Contrary to popular belief the 12 steps prove a closed mind leads to an opened heart.

29) A recovering 12 stepper—an anonymous missionary.

30) 12 steps is a treatment program that when done on a consistent basis prevents the disease from spreading.

LIFE ISN'T ABOUT FINDING YOURSELF. LIFE IS ABOUT CREATING YOURSELF.

THE 12 STEPS-CONTINUED

31) Before you let go, ask God.

32) Eating like a horse can be a step up for some.

33) Want to live the 10 Commandments? Try the 12 steps.

34) When all else fails, try the steps.

35) The 12-step program: taking ancient principles to modern terms.

36) As straightforward as 1, 2, 3; acknowledge…believe…decide.

37) If at first you do not succeed, try the steps.

38) Spice up your food with step work.

39) For many success comes when they replace their food program with a food plan and a twelve-step program.

WHAT KIND OF DAY SHALL I CHOOSE TODAY?

Today I can complain about my health,
Or I can celebrate being alive.

Today I can moan that it is raining,
Or be joyful at all that grows from the rain.

Today I can regret all I don't have,
Or rejoice in everything I do.

Today I can mourn everything I have lost,
Or eagerly anticipate what's to come.

Today I can complain that I have to work,
Or celebrate having a job to go to.

Today I can resent the mess the kids make,
Or give thanks that I have a family.

Today I can whine about the housework,
Or celebrate having a home.

Today I can cry over those who don't care for me,
Or be happy loving and being loved by those who do.

I choose to have a good day!

MEETING ROOMS

1) In the rooms we find that insanity is changing something and expecting the same result.

2) It's strange—when you first come in you hear stories about good things.

3) It's where you learn to feel good about the bad.

4) In the rooms is where you learn to talk a good game.

5) In the rooms is where talk is not cheap.

6) In the rooms is where saying your piece brings you peace.

7) It's where people tell real-life stories about terrible things in such a way that it makes the people in the room happy.

8) It's where you can treat someone like dirt with love and tolerance.

9) It's where people go to hear stories about the good, the bad, and the ugly.

10) In the rooms is where you can hear yourself without speaking.

11) The way to get to a meeting room is to take the low road.

12) A place where despicable and shameful acts are applauded.

13) In the rooms is where the powerless become powerful.

14) In the rooms you learn that forgiveness is an act of self-love.

15) In the rooms you learn to tolerate intolerance.

16) In the rooms is where you are told true love stories.

STEP ONE satisfies our hunger for truth and awareness.

MEETING ROOMS-CONTINUED

17) In the rooms is where you find that the most important meeting is with yourself.

18) Meetings are where you meet yourself.

19) Meetings—where wounded birds flock together.

20) If you listen in on a 12-step meeting you find that the meetings are a series of re-meetings.

21) If you met someone outside the rooms and every time they spoke to you they would start by saying, "hi" and giving their name, you would think they were insane.

22) What I like about the 12-step meetings is that you can never be late and never leave early.

23) Meetings—where the undecided decide.

24) Meetings—where you get the good news from the big book.

25) It's a place where you can come in high and leave even higher.

26) It's a place where you come in low and leave high.

27) It is where you are taught to not listen, to stop thinking, and begin unlearning.

28) It is where I really learned not to listen.

29) It is where I really learned not to hear but to listen.

30) It is where I was taught not to think.

31) Meetings—a place to air your dirty laundry.

32) In the churches, synagogues, and meeting halls you hear the word of God. In the rooms you see the words of God.

33) You can find a meeting at the crossroads of heaven and hell.

34) In the rooms you find people giving people verbal food.

SERENITY PRAYER

God grant me the serenity
To accept the things I cannot change,
Courage to change the things I can,
And the wisdom to know the difference.

Living one day at a time;
Enjoying one moment at a time;
Accepting hardship as the pathway to peace.

Taking, as He did, this sinful world
As it is, not as I would have it;

Trusting that He will make all things
Right if I surrender to His will;

That I may be reasonably happy
In this life,
And supremely happy with Him
Forever in the next.

-Reinhold Niebuhr

MEETING ROOMS-CONTINUED

35) Program people power is a higher power than food power.

36) Go to meetings and get fed.

37) You will find fertile soil to plant your seeds on the meeting house grounds.

38) The miracle food given at the meetings works for all problem eaters, overeaters, bulimic, anorexic and others.

39) Meetings satisfy hunger for fellowship, and quench our thirst for friendship.

"When you come to the edge of all the light you know and are about to step off into the darkness of the unknown, faith is knowing one of two things will happen: There will be something solid to stand on or you will be taught to fly."

-*Author Unknown*

THE PROGRAM/FELLOWSHIP

1) When I came into the program I was in such bad shape I couldn't even fall off the wagon.

2) The program proves that being a bad example can be a good example.

3) The program teaches strange math—it's where you can exchange one thought for another and make a whole.

4) In the program you fill the holes to become whole.

5) It's where you can treat someone like dirt with love and tolerance.

6) It's where the insane go to get sane.

7) The program takes those who have risen above the crowd and brings them back to earth.

8) The people in the program took the low road to get to the high road.

9) Instead of rubbing elbows you learn to touch hearts.

10) The magic of the program is that you end up feeling good about your bad deeds.

11) The program takes you to the far side of insanity.

12) The program is like Disneyland—there is something for everyone to enjoy.

GRATITUDE AND APPRECIATION

Any and all compliments can be handled by simply saying, "Why, thank you" (though it helps if you say it with a Southern accent).

Appreciation is a wonderful thing; it makes what is excellent in others belong to us as well. (Voltaire)

Be glad of life because it gives you the chance to love and to work and to play and to look at the stars. (Henry Van Dyke)

Be happy while you're living, for you're a long time dead. (Scottish proverb)

The best and most beautiful things in this world cannot be seen or even heard, but must be felt with the heart. (Helen Keller)

Blessed are those who can give without remembering and take without forgetting.

The capacity of delight is the gift of paying attention. (Julia Cameron)

A cloudy day is no match for a sunny disposition. (William Arthur Ward)

Don't cry because it's over; smile because it happened.

Don't ever save anything for a special occasion. Being alive is the special occasion.

THE PROGRAM/FELLOWSHIP-CONTINUED

13) The program is like a zoo—you get to see real animals.

14) The program is about embracing your insanity to get sane.

15) If you are in the rooms year after year and are not doing the steps you are actually stepping on the program.

16) The program is nonresistance in action.

17) In the program you come in thinking you're sane. The program immediately starts off by convincing you that you are insane. Next they ask you to embrace your insanity, and finally you finish by being grateful for your insanity. Now that's insane.

18) Many people come into the rooms wanting to get a jump on it. The program tells them to take it easy.

19) Some people in the program got there because they tried to captain two ships at the same time.

20) Many in the program say they are recovering Catholics. I say I am a recovering alcoholic and compulsive overeater who is Catholic.

21) The program—collective deroaching.

22) The program—collective debugging. (John Moser)

23) The program works much better if you do not ask what it can do for you, but rather ask what you can do for it.

FRIENDSHIP

"The better part of one's life consists of his friendships."
  -*Abraham Lincoln*

"A true friend is one who overlooks your failures and tolerates your success."
  -*Anonymous*

"The road to a friend's house is never long."
  -*Danish proverb*

"Books and friends should be few but good."

"A friend in need is a friend indeed."
  -*Latin proverb*

"Do not use a hatchet to remove a fly from your friend's forehead."
  -*Chinese proverb*

"The death of a friend is equivalent to the loss of a limb."
  -*German proverb*

"Life without a friend is like death without a witness."
  -*Spanish proverb*

"The best mirror is an old friend."

THE PROGRAM/FELLOWSHIP CONTINUED

24) The program asks you for commitments and upon keeping those, the program gives you what it promises.

25) A program of mutual commitment.

26) In the program you are not asked to try, but to work.

27) You learn in the program what works is work.

28) The only requirement to be a member of a 12-step program is a desire to stop. The only requirement for recovery is a willingness to go to any length.

29) The program teaches you to own your problems so that your problems do not own you.

30) The program is actually about reprogramming.

31) A program result, because you are heard, you can then be quiet, and hear the word of God.

32) The medicine prescribed by the program brings you relief from your disease. It is not for everyone. Consult with your sponsor to see if the 12 steps are for you. Side effects are peace, joy, love, serenity, happiness, and a loving God.

33) The program takes you from know-it-all to one who knows that he does not know it all and is content with not knowing it all, and knowing who knows it all.

"May there always be work for your hands to do, may your purse always hold a coin or two. May the sun always shine on your windowpane, may a rainbow be certain to follow each rain. May the hand of a friend always be near you, may God fill your heart with gladness to cheer you."

-Irish blessing

THE PROGRAM/FELLOWSHIP-CONTINUED

34) A program of reciprocal promises.

35) Working the program halfway is akin to reaching middle ground—you may be out of immediate danger but if you do not move to high ground you will soon be wet.

36) A fellowship of believers who trust in God and that they will receive a gift in order to give it away.

37) Other program tools—a hammer, an air compressor, a drill, a broom, and a jackhammer.

38) The program is about changing your thinking from over-thinking to rethinking.

39) Program instruments—a drum, a horn, and a fiddle.

40) A program that takes a person out of his mind and his world.

41) The program is like a magnet—it works on the law of attraction.

42) You commit to the program and the program commits to you.

43) A paradox of the program is that when you stop trying and start working, the program works.

44) Secret society where secrets are told and kept.

45) The program is about turning the tide.

46) Writing satisfies hunger for clarity, and quenches thirst for recording.

47) Literature satisfies hunger for guidance and quenches thirst for information.

48) Telephone satisfies hunger for a response to a call for help, and quenches the thirst for those hard to handle situations.

THE PROGRAM SATISFIES ONE'S HUNGER FOR:

Self-worth through service

Peace by doing the steps

Freedom by turning it over to God

Happiness by the fellowship and God connection

Human connection through the fellowship

Know serenity through action

Usefulness through sponsorship

Economic security through following God's will

Handling baffling situations by letting God help

THE PROGRAM/FELLOWSHIP-CONTINUED

49) Food plan satisfies hunger for simplicity and quenches the thirst for freedom from obsession.

50) Program acceptance... accepting the unacceptable.

51) If you follow it, it follows you.

52) When you get behind the program, the program will get behind you and push you through tough times.

53) Half measures do not work in the program; measuring half of the food before you eat works.

54) Many of us come into the program all stirred up, and the program settles us down.

55) Program tools—a blender, a strainer, and an apron.

56) Some in the program need emotional inflation, some need emotional deflation before physical inflation or deflation occurs.

57) Tap dancing through the program is not doing the footwork.

58) Where people feed each other verbally.

59) Overeaters anonymous- a way of life that enables one to find relief from compulsive eating.

60) A program heavyweight—one who has lost the desired amount of weight and has kept it off.

61) In the program you learn to love your enemy. Just ask any recovering person, and they will tell you how grateful they are for their disease. (Love your enemy).

62) A program of action. Intention without action leads to delusion.

HOW THE PROGRAM FEEDS US:

It satisfies our hunger for appreciation

It satisfies our hunger for acceptance

It satisfies our hunger for the wanted to be heard

It satisfies our hunger for self-acceptance

It satisfies our hunger for health

THE PROGRAM/FELLOWSHIP-CONTINUED

63) A program of indirect action- the action you take in other areas of your life positively affects your disease.

64) The program teaches us to take one bite at a time, finishing it before you take the next bite.

65) The program is about not biting off more than you can chew, and not chewing more than you need.

66) The program teaches you to become the student of god, rather than the listener of your chattering voices.

67) A central theme of O/A: no man is an island.

68) Food substitutes… the phone, the pen, the literature, meetings, service.

69) The program makes big men in smaller bodies.

70) Boot camp: 90 in 90.

71) The program teaches us to focus less on our weight, and more on weighting our goals.

72) I traded in my membership in a diet club for the fellowship of the program.

73) A program paradox: where giving up is success.

74) A program paradox: you must gain wait to lose weight.

75) You are encouraged to use "I" statements, which is the opposite of what you were taught.

76) For optimum health, most nutritionists recommend taking supplements in addition to your food. The program also suggests that you take supplements in addition to your food.

77) The question to ask is, "Am I in recovery, or is my disease?"

78) A slip occurs when your disease attempts recovery.

STEP ONE is simple: All people are powerless over food.

THE PROGRAM/FELLOWSHIP-CONTINUED

79) Recovery needs attending to or it soon disappears.

80) Tools of recovery for your disease… denial, rationalization, isolation, self-pity, self-centeredness, guilt, resentment.

81) In the program is where the spiritual meets the physical and gets emotional.

82) It's a program where you get bigger when you lose weight.

83) Program's other tools… a can opener, spatula, tongs, and a nutcracker.

84) The program paradox for me is that the smaller I get, the bigger I become.

85) The program takes you from closed-heartedness, and closed-mindedness, to openheartedness and open-mindedness.

86) Program snack foods: affirmations, quotes, and sayings.

87) All of your hard work will eventually be eaten up by your disease unless you get program help to overcome it.

88) After the final diet comes a food plan and that is what recovery is based on.

89) Let go then grab God.

90) The program teaches you that less is indeed more.

IN THE WORDS OF GEORGE BERNARD SHAW, PARAPHRASED:

"This is the true joy in life—

Being used for a purpose, recognized by yourself as a mighty one.

Being a force of nature, instead of a feverish, selfish little clod of ailments and grievances, complaining that the world will not devote itself to making you happy.

I AM OF THE OPINION THAT MY RECOVERY BELONGS TO THE WHOLE COMMUNITY AND AS LONG AS I LIVE IT IS MY PRIVILEGE TO DO FOR IT WHATEVER I CAN.

I WANT TO BE THOROUGHLY USED UP WHEN I DIE.

For the harder I work the more I live.

I rejoice in life for its own sake.

Life is no longer the brief candle it was when I was addicted.

It's a sort of splendid torch, which I've got to hold up for the moment and I want to make it burn as brightly as possible before handing it on to future generations of recovery."

RECOVERY

1) You are recovering when you reach the other side of insanity.

2) You are recovering when you near the side of sanity. (John Moser)

3) Recovery—a grateful compulsive eater.

4) A recovering Catholic is one who uses the program to have love and tolerance with the church and uses the principles of the program in their religious affairs.

5) Believing that you have recovered is the start of your relapse.

6) It is the only recovery program in which you are not expected to fully recover.

7) Recovery comes when you hear another voice.

8) Do you see it as a spiritual program of recovery or is it a program of spiritual recovery?

9) Abstinence allows one to begin their emotional and spiritual recovery.

10) Recovery is an attitude of gratitude with fortitude.

11) Recovery is action that believes in itself.

12) Recovery—what matters over the mind.

13) Recovery starts with a doubt in your mind.

14) The best eating contest is one that acknowledges the winners for having a normal weight.

15) Recovery… when your hunger for life becomes more important than food.

16) Some go from recovery to relapse, some relapse into recovery, and others recover into recovery.

17) Trading true reasons for good reasons is what honesty is about.

18) Plant good seeds in your mind and you will feed it well tomorrow.

Fast on fear; feast on faith.

Fast on self-pity and feast on gratitude.

Fast on fear and know that you can feast on courage.

Fast on isolation; feast on fellowship.

Fast on doubt; feast on belief.

Fast on self-will; feast on God's will.

Fast on criticism; feast on praise.

Fast on resentment; feast on forgiveness.

Fast on sadness; feast on happiness.

Fast on regret; feast on appreciation.

Fast on upset; feast on serenity.

Fast on conflict; feast on peace.

Fast on insecurity; feast on security.

RECOVERY-CONTINUED

19) Be like a nut and have a breakthrough.

20) Life is like an onion-- you peel it one layer at a time and sometimes you weep. And like an onion, each layer can bring you new life.

21) Recovery: either you have it or your disease has it.

22) I relapsed into recovery.

23) For some people it's relapse into recovery.

24) The taste of recovery is sweeter than honey.

25) Exchange some of the meat and potatoes for love and tolerance.

26) I am a much bigger man since I began my recovery in '91.

27) Anorexic, like the alcoholic, must hit her bottom before recovery starts.

28) Real magic: one loses food just by looking at it.

29) It takes more strength to put down than to pick up.

30) Relapse... when you decide to take back control of the uncontrollable.

31) Recovery comes when letting go is the right thing to do, and you do not argue, and when holding on is God's will and you obey.

32) Taking the miracle mile, going to any length to recover.

33) The miracle mile... when you go to any length to recover.

34) Recovery: thought for food.

35) The acid test: if you are not giving it away you haven't gotten it.

36) Disease... not at ease.

37) The problem may be that we are not taking what works for recovery, but rather what works for our disease.

38) Recovery: when comfort food is no longer comfortable.

TO "LET GO" TAKES LOVE

To "let go" does not mean to stop caring,
It means I can't do it for someone else.

To "let go" is not to cut myself off, it is
The realization I can't control another.

To "let go" is not to enable, but to allow
learning from natural consequences.

To "let go" is to admit powerlessness, which
means the outcome is not in my hands.

To "let go" is not to try to change or blame
another, it is to make the most of myself.

To "let go" is not to care for, but to care about.
To "let go" is not to fix, but to be supportive.
To "let go" is not to judge, but to allow another
to be a human being.

To "let go" is not to be in the middle arranging all the
outcomes, but to allow others to affect their own destinies.

To "let go" is not to be protective, it is to
permit another to face reality.

To "let go" is not to deny, but to accept.
To "let go" is not to nag, scold, or argue, but instead
to search out my own shortcomings and to correct them.

To "let go" is not to adjust everything to my desires, but to take each day as
it comes,
and to cherish myself in it.

To "let go" is not to criticize and regulate anybody
but to try to become what I dream I can be.

To "let go" is to not regret the past,
but to grow and to live for the future.
To "let go" is to fear less and to love more.

-Source Unknown

STEP NUMBER ONE

No man is an island
No man is an island
No man is an island
No man is an island
No man is an island
No man is an island
No man is an island
No man is an island
No man is an island
No man is an island

I cannot do it alone
I cannot do it alone
I cannot do it alone
I cannot do it alone
I cannot do it alone
I cannot do it alone
I cannot do it alone
I cannot do it alone
I cannot do it alone
I cannot do it alone

FORGIVE US OUR DEBTS

Loose the cords of mistakes binding us,
As we release the strands we hold
Of others' guilt.

Forgive our hidden past, the secret shames
As we consistently forgive
What others hide.

Lighten our load of secret debts as
We relieve others of their
Need to repay.

Erase the inner marks our failures make,
Just as we scrub our hearts
Of others' faults.

Absorb our frustrated hopes and dreams,
As we embrace those of others
With emptiness.

Untangle the knots within
So that we can mend our hearts'
Simple ties to others.

Compost our inner, stolen fruit
As we forgive others the spoils of
Their trespassing.

Loose the cords of mistakes binding us,
As we release the strands we hold
Of others' guilt.

STEP NUMBER TWO

It can happen
It can happen
It can happen
It can happen
It can happen
It can happen
It can happen
It can happen
It can happen
It can happen
It can happen
It can happen
It can happen
It can happen
It can happen

Step two satisfies our hunger for hope.

EMPTIED OF MYSELF

Sever me from myself that I may be grateful to you;

May I perish to myself that I may be safe in you;

May I die to myself that I may live in you;

May I wither to myself that I may blossom in you;

May I be emptied of myself that I may abound in you;

May I be nothing to myself that I may be all to you.

-Erasmus

STEP NUMBER THREE

1) An abstinent thought

2) Making a promise to the program

3) Soul power

4) Perpetual power

5) Thou shall have but one spirit within you.

6) I have surrendered to one spirit—the Holy Spirit.

7) The easiest way to resolve your thinking issue is to put your thoughts second to the will of God.

8) Step three satisfies our hunger for help.

KNOW MYSELF

I thank you Lord for knowing
Me better than I know myself,

And for letting me know myself
Better than others know me.

Make me, I ask you then, better
Than they suppose,

And forgive me for what they do not know.

-Abu Bakr

STEP NUMBER FOUR

1) Requires you to go backward to go forward.

2) Requires you to look backward in order to go forward. (John Moser)

3) Inventory is a spiritual balance sheet.

4) It is about uncovering your steps.

5) It is the crane that clears away life's wreckage and allows you to begin rebuilding.

6) The untold story

7) Writing your wrongs

8) After you have gone down the yellow brick road you can take the road to recovery back home.

9) To take the recovery path you must take steps.

10) Clear away the wreckage of your past; in step 9 you salvage it.

11) Step four satisfies our hunger for inner cleansing.

12) Step four: stirring the pot.

13) Step #4 is like peeling an orange-- you must remove the outer layer to get at the fruit.

NO EASY ANSWERS

May God bless me with discomfort at easy answers,

Half truths, and superficial relationships,

So that I may live deep within my heart.

And may God bless me with tears for those

Who suffer from pain, rejection and starvation, and war,

So that I may reach out my hand to comfort them.

And to turn their pain into joy.

-Anonymous

STEP NUMBER FIVE

1) Go where you have not gone before.

2) Letting the cat out of the bag.

3) Fifth step: Spilling the beans on yourself.

4) Step five satisfies our hunger to disclose the undiscloseable.

5) Confession: doing step five over and over.

DIFFICULTIES

It is not easy:

To apologize,

To being over,

To be unselfish,

To take advice,

To admit error,

To face sneers,

To be charitable,

To avoid mistakes,

To keep on trying,

To be considerate,

To endure success,

To profit by mistakes,

To forgive and forget,

To think and then act,

To keep out of the rut,

To make the best of little,

To subdue an unruly temper,

To maintain a high standard,

To shoulder a deserved blame,

To recognize a silver lining.

But it always pays!

STEP NUMBER SIX

Opened arms
Opened arms
Opened arms
Opened arms
Opened arms
Opened arms
Opened arms
Opened arms
Opened arms
Opened arms

Step six satisfies our hunger for God's help.

THE PRAYER OF ST. FRANCIS

Lord, make me a channel of thy peace,

That where there is hatred, I may bring love;

That where there is wrong, I may bring the spirit of forgiveness;

That where there is discord, I may bring harmony;

That where there is error, I may bring truth;

That where there is doubt, I may bring faith;

That where there is despair, I may bring hope;

That where there are shadows, I may bring light;

That where there is sadness, I may bring joy.

Lord, grant that I may seek rather to comfort than to be comforted;

To understand, than to be understood;

To love, than to be loved.

For it is by self-forgetting that one finds.

It is by forgiving that one is forgiven.

It is by dying that one awakens to Eternal Life.

STEP NUMBER SEVEN

Validates the power of prayer

On your knees

Ask humbly; listen honestly

I ask humbly and listen honestly; God's will becomes very clear.

Ask humbly; listen honestly and you will clearly see.

Step number 7: Eat humble pie.

Step seven satisfies our hunger for God's help.

VOICE IN THE WINDS

O Great Spirit,
Whose voice I hear in the winds
And whose breath gives life
To all the world,
Hear me! I am small and weak.
I need your strength and wisdom.
Let me walk in beauty
And make my eyes
Ever behold the sunset.
Make my hands respect the things
You have made.
And my ears sharp to hear your voice.
Make me wise
So that I may understand
The things you have taught my people.
Let me learn the lessons
You have hidden in every leaf and rock.
I seek strength,
Not to be greater than my brother,
But to fight my greatest enemy—myself.
Make me always ready to come to you
With clean hands and straight eyes.
So when life fades, as the fading sunset,
My spirit may come to you without shame.

STEP NUMBER EIGHT

The "did-to" list
The "did-to" list
The "did-to" list
The "did-to" list
The "did-to" list
The "did-to" list
The "did-to" list
The "did-to" list
The "did-to" list
The "did-to" list

Step 8 satisfies our hunger for awareness and willingness.

THE RIGHT ROAD

O Lord God,

I have no idea where I am going,

I do not see the road ahead of me,

I cannot know for certain where it will end.

Nor do I really know myself.

And the fact that I think I am following your will

Does not mean that I am actually doing so.

But I believe that the desire to please you

Does in fact please you.

And I hope I have that desire in all that I am doing.

...I will trust you always

Though I may seem to be lost

And in the shadow of death

I will not fear,

And you are ever with me,

And you will never leave me

To make my journey alone.

STEP NUMBER NINE

1) It is important not to step on anyone.

2) Teaches you that telling the truth may not always be the right thing to do.

3) Telling the truth may not always be right. (John Moser)

4) He is a normal person in his own mind.

5) Desire earns you a seat in the rooms; taking the steps keeps placing you there.

6) Getting on your knees is encouraged to help you pray; getting up is encouraged to help you stay.

7) The steps actually work on you, but at first you must work them.

8) Working the steps is like kneading dough; if you keep doing it you will eventually rise.

9) Where the journey begins after the final step.

I RISE TODAY

I rise today through

God's strength to pilot me,

God's eye to look before me,

God's ear to hear me,

God's word to speak for me,

God's hand to guard me,

God's way to lie before me,

God's shield to protect me,

God's hosts to save me

From the snares of the devil,

From everyone who desires me ill

From afar or near, alone or in a crowd.

-Saint Patrick

STEP NUMBER NINE-CONTINUED

10) The least valid statement in the program: I have finished the steps.

11) You are finished once you finish with the steps.

12) One of the goals of the program is to awaken the spirit and to put to bed the suffering.

13) A spiritual awakening occurs when you stop shooting the messenger and receive the message.

14) If you are going to shoot the messenger at least wait until the message has been delivered.

15) Traditions 8: we are a bunch of amateurs.

16) Step Number 9 promises you that life will be a cup of cherries.

17) Amends: when the mind tells the body the exact nature of its wrongs to the body and the body accepts.

Step nine satisfies our hunger for peace and forgiveness.

TEACH ME TO SING

Giver of Life, Creator of all that is lovely

Teach me to sing the words of your song.

I want to feel the music of living

And not fear the sad songs

Composed of both laughter and tears.

Teach me to dance to the sounds of your world

And your people

I want to move in rhythm with your plan.

Help me to follow your leading

To risk even falling

To rise and keep trying

Because you are leading the dance.

-Author unknown

STEP NUMBER TEN

1) Is six steps in one

2) Made up of smaller steps

3) Is a dance you do everyday

4) Is the Texas two-step

5) Is the exception to the rule

6) One step at a time except for step ten

7) If you find yourself too busy on the tenth step to get to steps 11 and 12 you may need to make more amends.

8) An act of daily reflection, confession, and amends

9) An admission that even with all the step work you will find that you will continue to do wrong on occasion

10) A recognition of the fact that in spite of making a decision to turn our will and our lives over to the care of God, and of having done the steps, you will continue to make mistakes

11) The whetstone that keeps you sharp

12) When 4 and 5 make 10

13) Perpetual confession

14) Tenth step: amends for the religious and spiritual; amen, amen, amen.

15) Tenth step amends for the atheist... encore, encore, encore.

16) Tenth step amends for the agnostic... we, we, we.

17) Step Ten satisfies our daily hunger.

18) Step 10 feeds us everyday.

FOR TODAY

O God:

Give me strength to live another day;

Let me not turn coward before its difficulties;

Let me not lose faith in other people;

Keep me sweet and sound of heart,

In spite of ingratitude, treachery, or meanness;

Preserve me from minding little stings or giving them;

Help me to keep my heart clean,

And so to live so honestly and fearlessly

That no outward failure can dishearten me or take away the joy of

conscious integrity;

Open wide the eyes of my soul that I may see good in all things;

Grant me this day some new vision of thy truth;

Inspire me with the spirit of joy and gladness;

And make me the cup of strength to suffering souls;

In the name of the strong Deliverer,

Our only Lord and Savior, Jesus Christ.

STEP NUMBER ELEVEN

1) We see the wisdom when it's said through prayer and meditation.

2) Requires that you do more than pray.

3) Pray for the willingness to meditate before step 11.

4) Wisdom can be seen more effectively when we look at the numbers separately, 1 is for prayer and 1 for meditation; both are needed.

5) The contrarian eleventh step—silent prayer speaking meditation.

6) Unconscious contact with God—when good things happen to you and you say, "What happened?"

7) Message morphs when you have many messengers.

8) Saying grace with the 11th step in the back round improves our ability to choose the right food in the right quantity.

9) Prayer and meditation are nectar for the soul.

10) For me a balanced meal includes step 11.

11) Step 11 satisfies our hunger to know our creator.

PERSISTENCE

Nothing in the world can take the place of persistence.

Talent will not; nothing is more common than unsuccessful men with talent.

Genius will not; unrewarded genius is almost a proverb.

Education will not; the world is full of educated derelicts.

Persistence and determination alone are omnipotent.

-Calvin Coolidge

STEP NUMBER TWELVE

Spiritual awakening occurs after the mind is quieted and the ego is put to sleep.

Spiritual awakening occurs after the mind is quieted and the ego is put to sleep.

Spiritual awakening occurs after the mind is quieted and the ego is put to sleep.

Spiritual awakening occurs after the mind is quieted and the ego is put to sleep.

Spiritual awakening occurs after the mind is quieted and the ego is put to sleep.

Spiritual awakening occurs after the mind is quieted and the ego is put to sleep.

Spiritual awakening occurs after the mind is quieted and the ego is put to sleep.

Spiritual awakening occurs after the mind is quieted and the ego is put to sleep.

Spiritual awakening occurs after the mind is quieted and the ego is put to sleep.

Spiritual awakening occurs after the mind is quieted and the ego is put to sleep.

Step 12 satisfies our hunger to help others.

PROGRAM PSALMS

"Amazing Grace"

"Nearer My God to Thee"

"We Call on Him"

"I Walk in the Garden Alone"

"Standing on the Promises"

"My Prayer"

"All I Have to Do Is Dream"

"How Great Thou Art"

"It's All in His Hands"

"Peace in the Valley"

"You Are My Sunshine"

PEACE

It does not mean to be in a place where there is no noise, trouble, or hard work. It means to be in the midst of those things and still be calm in your heart.

-Unknown

PROGRAM PROVERBS

1) Serenity, letting go, and helping God.

2) Skipping steps keeps you off balance.

3) Enlightenment springs from the manure of the mind.

4) Take a tip from the big book and revise yourself.

5) Honesty is about uncovering your tracks.

6) Will power and want power give way to higher power.

7) Put your disease at ease, and when it is at ease it's no longer a disease.

8) You cannot do the steps sitting on your high horse.

9) Exchange the food and drink for love and tolerance.

10) Tolerance is when the tolerant tolerate the intolerant until the intolerant become tolerant.

11) Getting high brings you to the bottom.

12) Insanity—choosing your lower power.

13) When you receive, don't ask.

14) Most apples are bad.

15) A great example can be good or bad.

16) What is the cost of a free ticket?

17) It is possible to get good fruit from a bad tree.

PROGRAM PROVERBS CONTINUED

1) A soft answer turneth away wrath: but grievous words stir up anger.

2) The tongue of the wise useth knowledge aright: but the mouth of fools poureth out foolishness.

3) The eyes of the LORD are in every place, beholding the evil and the good.

4) A wholesome tongue is a tree of life: but perverseness therein is a breach in the spirit.

5) A fool despiseth his father's instruction: but he that regardeth reproof is prudent.

6) In the house of the righteous is much treasure: but in the revenues of the wicked is trouble.

7) The lips of the wise disperse knowledge: but the heart of the foolish doeth not so.

8) The sacrifice of the wicked is an abomination to the LORD: but the prayer of the upright is his delight.

9) The way of the wicked is an abomination unto the LORD: but he loveth him that followeth after righteousness.

10) Correction is grievous unto him that forsaketh the way: and he that hateth reproof shall die.

11) Hell and destruction are before the LORD: how much more then the hearts of the children of men?

12) A scorner loveth not one that reproveth him: neither will he go unto the wise.

13) A merry heart maketh a cheerful countenance: but by sorrow of the heart the spirit is broken.

PROGRAM PROVERBS-CONTINUED

18) You cannot hit a home run sitting in the bleachers.

19) Highest power: when God's will and your will are perfectly aligned.

20) Work works.

21) The baptism of your rebirth

22) HALT: happy, aligned, loving, and tolerant.

23) GO: god only.

24) A sponsor: the minister of the word.

25) A prayer a day helps keep the doctor away.

26) It takes a heart to open a heart.

27) The food of love makes you feast on life.

28) Recovery starts when the arguing stops.

29) Recovery: when you lose.

30) Platinum became more precious than gold because of its usefulness.

31) The road even less traveled

32) Serenity: finding a round hole for your round peg.

33) Spiritual minds think alike.

34) Think less; do more.

35) GRACE: God Remove All Compulsive Eating

36) The best way to hang in there is to let go.

37) Love is a food that feeds all.

38) The food of love makes you feast on life.

ALTERNATE SERENITY PRAYER

God grant me the serenity to accept the people I cannot change
directly,

The courage to change the person I can,

The wisdom to know that person is I,

And to leave the changes of others to God and them.

PROGRAM PROVERBS-CONTINUED

39) Food for thought... thoughtful food.

40) Soothing music is snack food for the spirit.

41) Make your first course... a spiritual one.

42) Cleanse your spiritual palate with amends/confession.

43) Kindness: fruit for the soul.

44) The fruits of one's lips are the dessert for the mind and soul.

45) Feeding others feeds your soul.

46) Letting go allows one to hold on.

47) Freedom from self-imprisonment requires one to let go.

48) Some of the hardest things to let go of are the things that one cannot really hold on to.

49) PROGRAM SLOGANS: 1. Take what works and leave the rest (stay away from your trigger food.) 2. Easy does it (go light on the portions). 3 Keep it simple (no fixings). 4. One bite at a time. 5. Let (the food) go and let god.

50) The twelve important words: God, love, tolerance, service, honesty, willingness, humility, work, gratitude, progress, prayer, and meditation.

51) The twelve least important words: me me me me me me me me me me me me.

52) Dessert for the soul... kind words.

53) Sarcasm... emotional junk food.

Biggest Handicap- Fear

Most Beautiful Day- Today

Easiest Thing to Do- Give Up

Biggest Error- To Quit

Biggest Fault- Self-Centeredness

Best Gift- Faith

Greatest Need- Good Sense

Worst Sentiment- Jealousy

Best Present- A Pardon

Best Christian- Mary

Most Beautiful Thing in the World- Love

TRADITIONS

1) Tradition 1: United we stand, divided we fall.

2) Tradition 2: When two or more are gathered in my name.

3) Tradition 3: Unconditional acceptance.

4) Tradition 4: Guided by God only.

5) Tradition 5: Minister.

6) Tradition 6: To each his own.

7) Tradition 7: A bunch of amateurs.

8) Tradition 8: Disorganization is the key to success.

9) Tradition 9: I hear nothing, I say nothing, and I see nothing.

10) Tradition 10: Behind closed doors.

11) Tradition 11: A closed-door session.

12) Tradition 12: A secret society helping a select few.

13) Tradition 13: Anonymity satisfies hunger for security and quenches the thirst for privacy.

MIRACLES ARE EVERYWHERE

Miracles are not only
Ecstatic visions or holy
Interventions
Visited upon the chosen few.

Every moment we are alive
Is full of reasons to sing
Out in joyful gratitude.

Every breath we are given
Is a reminder that
The glory of life is at hand.

In the people we love,
In the beauty of nature,
In the golden sun
That rises each morning-
Miracles are everywhere.

MIRACLES

M Mary Martha Melissa Megan Marsha Melinda Matilda
   Maureen

I Irene Isabelle Ida Ilene Ingrid Iris Irma Ivonna Ivanka Ivory
   Ivy

R Rachael Rose Robin Rhoda Rita Rochelle Ronnie Rosa
   Rosalyn Ruth

A Ann Alice Amy Alisa Annette Alicia Ava Alvira Alyson
   Amanda

C Carol Carla Cindy Cathy Christine Caroline Carmella
   Carey Candy

L Linda Lisa Louise Lorie Lucia Lee Liz Laura Lola Lindsey
   Lea

E Ellen Elizabeth Evyone Evett Eileen Eve Eleanor Ethel
   Edythe

S Sally Susan Sara Sophia Sabrina Sandy Samantha Sandra

M Michael Martin Murray Mickey Mark Malcolm
   Manuel Morris

I Ines Ingram Irving Irvin Isaac Isaiah Issa Ishmael Israel
   Igore Ivan

R Richard Robert Rolland Ryan Russell Randy Ricky Randall
   Rusty

A Albert Alan Art Amos Alex Aladdin Alexander Alfred Alec

C Carl Charles Clark Chris Carmon Chuck Craig Carlo
   Christian

L Louie Lincoln Larry Lonny Lenny Lawrence Lionel Lucky
   Lou

E Edward Edwin Evert Evan Ellis Evin Edgar Eddy

S Samuel Sammy Scott Stuart Stanley Sandy Sean Sal Shawn

THIRD STEP PRAYER

God,

I offer myself to Thee

To build with me and to do with me as Thou wilt.

Relieve me of the bondage of self, that I may better do Thy will.

Take away my difficulties, that victory over them may bear witness

To those I would help of Thy Power, Thy love and Thy way of life.

May I do Thy will always!

PRAYER AND MEDITATION

1) When praying remember to stop and meditate so that you may hear the answer to your prayer.

2) God told us to pray and meditate in order that we can ask and receive.

3) Ask through prayer and receive through meditation.

4) Often we ask to get and seldom we ask to give.

5) Careful you are not so busy praying for answers that you do not hear the response.

6) Praying is good; praying with meditation is better.

7) Powerful prayer is praying for the ones you love and the ones you do not.

8) If you start your day on your knees and end your day on your knees that is very good; by adding the act of sitting quietly for God's word it becomes better.

9) Meditation proves that sitting on your rear can be the most effective move you can make.

ASK AND YOU SHALL RECEIVE. HERE IS HOW IT WORKS. BEFORE YOU TAKE THAT FIRST BITE, ASK GOD IF THAT IS HIS WILL FOR YOU TO EAT WHAT YOU WANT TO EAT. IF GOD SAYS NO AND IT'S NOT GOOD FOR YOU, THEN YOU HAVE RECEIVED.

If God says yes and it's good for you in kind and quantity, then you have received. If you begin to eat the wrong thing and stop before finishing, then you have received. And finally, if at first you do not eat when you should, then start, you have received.

PRAYER AND MEDITATION-CONTINUED

10) Prayer and belief go hand in hand; prayer without belief is but a wish.

11) How strange; at first you admit your powerlessness, then you pray for power to your higher power.

12) God grant me the serenity to accept that I cannot eat all that I want, the courage to ask for your help to stop when I'm full, and the wisdom to know that my life is at stake.

13) Serenity... peace, forgiveness.

14) The palate of the soul is pleased by the many flavors of prayer.

15) Dear God give us this day our daily bread, and forgive us for taking the whole loaf; protect us from gluttony. Amen.

16) One of the best ways to help yourself in between meals is with prayer.

17) Meditation: a mindless act.

18) Meditation: a main course for the soul.

19) Prayers... soul food.

TWELFTH STEP PRAYER

Dear God,

My spiritual awakening continues to unfold.

The help I have received I shall pass on and give to others,
Both in and out of the Fellowship.

For this opportunity I am grateful.

I pray most humbly to continue walking
Day by day on the road of spiritual progress.

I pray for the inner strength and wisdom to practice

The principles of this way of life in all I do and say.

I need You, my friends, and the program every hour of every day.

This is a better way to live.

THE TWELVE STEPS IN TWELVE MINUTES

Doing the twelve steps in twelve minutes:

"Dear Lord, I have made many mistakes. I'm tired of doing it wrong; I need your help, and I will follow You. I have hurt people along the way, especially you and I. I know that I have bad ways of being and stand ready for your miracle of grace. As I recount those I have hurt, I commit to you that from this day forward I will be vigilant about my actions and behavior; when I am wrong, I will confess to those I have wronged that day and to you. My prayer to You is to help me on my path, and to sit quietly so that my conscious contact with you expands."

LOVE

Love is a friendship that has caught fire. It is quiet understanding, mutual confidence, sharing and forgiving. It is a loyalty through good and bad. It settles for less than perfection and makes allowances for human weaknesses.

Love is content with the present, it hopes for the future and it doesn't brood over the past. It's the day-in and day-out chronicle of irritations, problems, compromises, small disappointments, big victories and working toward common goals.

If you have love in your life, it can make up for a great many things you lack. If you don't have it, no matter what else there is, it's not enough.

LOVE

1)   Love and tolerance are the twin railings for the 12-stepper to hold on to.

2)   Love: Tolerating the intolerant, until the intolerant become tolerant.

3)   Love is when the unlovable are loved through their un-lovability to lovability.

4)   Tough love is not really tough.

5)   Tough love is when you do not let love get in the way of doing what is best for someone.

6)   Acceptance—one part love, one part tolerance.

7)   If you have tolerance of someone they experience tolerance; if you add love to tolerance they experience acceptance.

8)   Add love to tolerance and you get acceptance.

9)   Love and tolerate others as you love and tolerate yourself.

10) The program proves that love alone is not enough. You can love someone and not accept them; you can tolerate someone and not accept them, but you cannot love and tolerate someone and not accept them.

11) Having love and tolerance of oneself brings true peace.

12) Acceptance is when love meets tolerance.

THE THINGS THAT COUNT

Count your garden by the flowers,
Never by the leaves that fall.

Count your days by garden hours,
Don't remember clouds at all.

Count your nights by stars, not shadows.

Count your years with smiles, not tears.

Count your blessings, not your troubles.

Count your age by friends, not by years.

GOD

1) Commitment—making God's will superior to how you think or feel.

2) Peace comes when you align your will with God's.

3) If you start slipping, check to make sure you are still holding God's hand.

4) God grant me the serenity to know that I cannot change other people, the courage to change the person I can and to have the wisdom to know that that person is I.

5) Hearing God through ordinary people.

6) The right has God; the left has a higher party, and the independent have love and tolerance.

7) You go from no power to high power to higher power to highest power.

8) You alone have no power; you and the group high power; God higher power; you and God the highest power for you.

9) God does not care what house you choose, as long as you choose a house that honors Him and respects others.

10) The God of your understanding does not change; just your understanding of Him.

11) The way you are asked to clean up your act is to first act as if, then act as God would.

12) Do you really want to find God's will?

13) It's a battle of wills—my will, their will, our will, God's will. You may win a battle or two but the only way to win the war is to side with God.

14) The one will that cannot be changed is God's will.

15) One will that you will get in trouble with when you challenge it is God's will.

16) Happy, joyous, and free; happy because of one's disease, joyous in spite of an incurable disease, and free because of not being normal.

17) My will, I will, their will, our will, your will.

18) WWGD? What would God do?

19) It is easier to let go when you see the gift.

IT'S ALWAYS A GOOD IDEA TO KEEP YOUR WORDS WARM
AND TENDER. YOU MAY HAVE TO EAT THEM SOMEDAY,
AND IF AND WHEN THAT DAY COMES, EATING YOUR WORDS
WILL NOT CAUSE YOU TO CHOKE ON THEM.

GOD-CONTINUED

20) The power of food can be overpowered by a higher power called God.

21) God: One who dishes out food for your soul.

22) The pantry of God is filled with healthy goodies.

23) Dear God, bless this food that it may nourish my body and soul.

24) Let go; get God.

25) When your desire to take the hand of God gets strong enough, letting go gets easier.

26) Are you sure that God wants you to let Go and let God?

27) Get your mind aligned with God. Get your mind off of self by doing for God and others.

28) Your time and God's time become one when you and God have the same watch (will).

29) Hold on and go with God.

30) As it relates to the program one must let God and never let go.

31) I have been given so many gifts from God that at times I no longer look for them, or I stop appreciating them, but rather focus on their gifts God gave others.

32) Eventually if you stop appreciating gifts from God he will stop sending them and will give to others.

33) God's will: food for thought.

34) I would rather do God's will and stumble again and again, than to do my will perfectly.

35) Freedom comes when you turn your will over to the care of God.

36) If your thoughts have you imprisoned, then why not try doing the will of God and free yourself from the prison of your thoughts?

37) Choosing to do God's will puts the proper order to things.

38) When God dwells in you, the kingdom of heaven is within.

39) At the crossroads of surrender, one surrenders to their disease or surrenders to God.

40) It appears that the true road less traveled is the road to God.

41) Make your second serving of God.

42) Let go and let God is good. Let go and get God is better.

"The universe is transformation; our life is what our thoughts make it."

-*Marcus Aurelius*

GOD-CONTINUED

43) Corrective lenses for the person with an eating disorder are ones in which you see through the eyes of God.

44) From the manure of the mind, when fed by God becomes the fertilizer that helps one grow into a peach of a man.

45) Happy, joyous and free… GOD's will.

46) God: a qualified health care professional.

47) GOD: the one who guides you through the jungles of life.

48) In the beginning life was good when Adam and Eve listened to God. Then they stopped. Life becomes good again when we listen to God.

49) Alternative medicine: God.

50) Self-help books require help from God to work.

51) You will have smooth sailing if you let your ship be guided by God.

52) God: spiritual food.

53) Dog: doing only God's work.

54) The missing ingredient in most diets: God.

55) If you spice up your meal with the will of God, your meal will nurture you.

56) Tasting the goodness of God suppresses your appetite.

57) If you make God the main ingredient in the food then the meal is good.

58) When the spirit is starved, the food is often used to feed it when all that is needed is God.

59) When God is dining with me, my meals nourish me.

60) The real heart-healthy food starts with God.

61) Let go of the food and give it to God.

62) As your cravings for God increase your craving for food decreases.

63) God is the medication that is prescribed to keep the disease of compulsive eating from spreading.

64) Try turning your excess food over to God.

65) Do not just put your eating obsession in God's hands, also out the excess.

WHAT IS MEDITATION?

Meditation is the activity of calling to mind, and thinking over, and dwelling on, and applying to oneself, the various things that one knows about the works and ways and purpose and promises of God.

It is an activity of holy thought, consciously performed in the presence of God, under the eye of God, by the help of God as a means of communication with God. Its purpose is to clear one's mental and spiritual vision of God, and to let His truth make its full and proper impact on one's mind and heart.

It is a matter of talking to oneself about God and oneself; it is, indeed, often a matter of arguing with oneself, reasoning oneself out of moods and doubts and unbelief into a clear apprehension of God's power and grace.

GOD-CONTINUED

66) GOD: grace of divinity.

67) Serenity prayer for Contrarians: God grant me the serenity to accept that I may not change, the courage to keep working to change, and the wisdom to continue changing.

68) Guru: GOD and you.

69) Guru: GOD and your sponsor.

70) God grant me the serenity to know that I'm a round peg and would not fit into a square hole, and that I need to find a round hole or be square.

71) God's gratitude list—when you write down God's will for you in all aspects of your life.

72) Just as ignorance of the law is no excuse, not knowing God's will is unwillingness.

73) When your will is willing then you will know God's will.

74) God's home in your heart.

75) Quieting the mind allows you to hear the word of God.

76) It is far better to know God's will and tell Him you are not yet ready than to keep asking Him for His will and later saying, "I don't know."

77) If the kingdom of heaven is within, then God's home is in your heart.

78) Peace comes when you align your will with God's.

79) From the manure of the mind, when fed by God, becomes the fertilizer that helps one grow into a peach of a man.

80) If your steps are not built on the foundation of God, then they will eventually crumble.

81) For me the 12 steps is about uncovering your tracks and walking in the footsteps of God.

82) If you walk in the footsteps of GOD long enough people will begin to see you as one who walks on water.

83) Do not forget you are gathered in His name.

84) Interesting… the word "Dog" is "God" backwards; the dog itself does not have it backwards, giving unconditional love, is being manageable.

A PRAYER FOR BLESSED ACCEPTANCE

Dear God, in this moment I hold your acceptance.

You love me completely, just as I am.

You see my great potential within,

And you nurture my tender heart of compassion.

In this moment, I let your acceptance be my own.

I accept others as the children of God.

I hold high their inner greatness,

Always seeking to serve the highest and best within all people.

And so it is.

HIGHER POWER

1) You learn to replace will power with higher power.

2) The right has God, the left has a higher power, and the independent have love and tolerance.

3) You go from no power to high power to higher power to highest power.

4) My will, I will, their will, our will, and your will.

5) We are all truly powerless over food and we are dependent on it. Without it we would die.

6) If you have trouble deciding, just decide to decide.

7) The cost to satisfy the emotional and spiritual hunger with food is higher than our higher power wants for us.

GRATITUDE IS THE HEART'S MEMORY

Gratitude unlocks the fullness of life. It turns what we have into enough, and more. It turns denial into acceptance, chaos into order, confusion into clarity. It turns problems into gifts, failures into success, the unexpected into perfect timing, and mistakes into important events. Gratitude makes sense of our past, brings peace for today and creates a vision for tomorrow.

SERVICE

1) The more determined you are to give it away the more it comes back to you.

2) Service is your gift back to God; your continued recovery is his way of thanking you.

3) Reaching out extends your hand; reaching in extends your heart.

4) To extend the hand requires you to reach out; to extend the heart requires you to reach in.

5) The three most important words in the program are service, service, and service.

6) Recovery is fed through service.

7) The words you give out can feed and nourish people or they can make them ill.

8) Service: passion fruit.

9) Service satisfies hunger for usefulness, and quenches the thirst for purpose.

BELIEVE

Believe in your questions, no matter how trifling.
They are the gateway to knowledge, wisdom and enlightenment.

Believe in your gifts, no matter how small; they are God's providence to your world,
To enrich it, to enable it, to bring it love.

Believe in your past, no matter how painful.
It is a unique book of history; Gospel Revelation of God's mercy and faithfulness.

Believe in your yearnings, no matter how subtle.
They are energy, urging you forward in your quest for God.

Believe in your sinlessness, no matter painted fingers.
They are only passing vestiges of fears,
Reminding you to forgive, to remain rooted in Love's reality.

Believe in your vision no matter the climb.
It is a mountain peak, calling you to experience God.

Believe in your ideas, no matter the doubts
They are seeds, seeking nourishment, sunshine, life-giving water.

Believe in your neighbor, no matter the risk,
Each one is sent from God to walk with you.

Believe in your God, no matter the mist.
God is strong and trustworthy and cares for you.

ALL:

May the God who creates,
The God who redeems and
The God who makes us all holy,
Bless us and remain with us
Forever and ever. Amen.

PROMISES

We are going to know a new freedom and a new happiness.

1) The end result of the steps is enlightened insanity.

2) What amazes many people is that a recovering person is happy about being not okay.

3) Speaking reveals your insanity, and upon speaking you become silent.

4) The bottom line of O.A. is that it transfers the angry, sad, and confused compulsive eater into a grateful one.

5) I am sorry for those of us who are normal as they are not free.

6) Are you restrained by the shackles of normalcy?

7) A miracle: only after people learn that they will not totally recover that they become happy, joyous, and free.

8) Happy, joyous, and free—happy because of one's disease, joyous in spite of an incurable disease, and free because of not being normal.

9) Physical recovery starts you on the road to happiness; emotional recovery makes it joyous and spiritual recovery sets you free.

10) The steps actually work on you, but at first you must work them.

11) One of the goals of the program is to awaken the spirit and to put to bed the suffering.

12) Five minutes of inspiration followed up with action is worth more than a lifetime of inaction.

13) Success comes one abstinent meal at a time.

14) Often the hunger we have cannot be satisfied with food.

I AM OKAY

I WILL READ EVERY DAY UNTIL THIS THINKING BECOMES
MY THINKING.

1. I feel warm towards ME because I am a unique, one-of-a-kind person; ever doing the best I can, ever growing in love and wisdom.
2. I am in charge of my life.
3. My first responsibility is to learn to love myself more and more. The more I love ME, the better I will love others.
4. I make my own decisions, take credit for the good ones and accept the consequences of the others, but always free of self-accusation, guilt, or remorse.
5. I am not my actions; I am the one who acts. I am a fallible human being, who sometimes acts in a good way, sometimes in a not-so-good way.
6. It's nice to have other people's love and approval, but even without it, I can love and accept MYSELF.
7. It is not what happens to me that determines whether I feel good or bad, but my attitude towards those things that does.
8. I do not have to prove my worth or excellence. I need only express myself as honestly and effectively as I can at any moment.
9. I am free of animosity or resentment.
10. I am a success to the degree that I feel warm and loving towards ME.
11. I am kind and gentle with ME.
12. I live one day at a time, doing first things first, one at a time, and second things second.
13. I am patient because I have the rest of my life to grow.
14. Every experience of my life contributes to my personal growth.
15. No one in the world is one bit more or less important than I.
16. My mistakes or failures just prove that I am human.

THE ABOVE ARE GOALS. IF I THINK RIGHT, I WILL FEEL RIGHT!

WE WILL NOT REGRET THE PAST NOR WISH TO SHUT THE DOOR ON IT

1) Part of the program is about being a bad example.

2) It's strange that talking to someone about the worst things you have done helps them.

3) Character defect shows up under the microscope of the steps.

4) Sometimes I am a bad example of someone being good and other times I'm a good example of someone being bad.

5) Real physical recovery requires you to go beyond stopping.

6) Real physical recovery requires you to stop compulsively eating and start exercising. (John Moser)

7) The good the bad and the ugly.

PHYSICAL NEEDS:
Food
Shelter
Water
Health
Rest
Elimination
Light
Sex

EMOTIONAL-PSYCHOLOGICAL NEEDS:
Affection
Understanding
Encouragement
Attention
Compliments
Compassion
Self-esteem
Fellowship
Be consulted
Respect
Acceptance
Friends
Responsibility
Fulfillment
Meaningful work
Privacy
Appreciation
Communication
Quiet

SPIRITUAL NEEDS:
Love
Hope
Faith
Wisdom
Knowledge
Peace
Trust
Principle of unity
Prayer
Worship
Meditation
Study

WE WILL COMPREHEND THE WORD "SERENITY" AND WE WILL KNOW PEACE

1)   Every time you do a step, you make a step towards recovery.

2)   It is where your blacklist is replaced with your gratitude list.

3)   Recovery starts when the arguing stops.

4)   Quieting the mind allows you to hear the word of God.

5)   If the kingdom of heaven is within, then God's home is in your heart.

6)   Once you let go you are free to bounce off the walls.

7)   In the program is where you are encouraged to get out of your head and into your heart.

THE TEN STEPS

1) Moving out of Denial into AWARENESS.

2) Moving out of Shock into FEELING.

3) Moving out of Hopelessness into CONFIDENCE.

4) Moving out of Fear into SAFETY.

5) Moving out of Anger into FORGIVENESS.

6) Moving out of Guilt into SELF-FORGIVENESS.

7) Moving out of Shame into SELF-APPRECIATION.

Having moved past the more "negative" states, one can then complete the more "positive" ones.

8) GRATITUDE and APPRECIATION.

9) LOVE

10) FAREWELL and RELEASE.

NO MATTER HOW FAR DOWN THE SCALE WE HAVE GONE, WE WILL SEE HOW OUR EXPERIENCE CAN BENEFIT OTHERS

1) The newcomer asks God to cure his problem; the old-timer thanks God for his problem.

2) In the twelve steps you learn that no one is 100% honest 100% of the time, but rather we have degrees of honesty.

3) A good story about something bad is better than a bad story about something good.

4) You learn to have good thoughts about something bad.

5) 12 step meetings—where you get to meet yourself.

6) The steps are the medications that arrest the disease.

7) You slip back into your disease when you fail to take your medication.

8) An enabler—one who loves someone to death.

9) In the rooms you meet a group of storytellers who know hundreds of stories and yet tell only one.

FIFTEEN WAYS TO BE MISERABLE

1. Wait for others to make you happy.

2. Blame everyone else for your unhappiness.

3. Use "if only" whenever you can regarding time, money, or friends.

4. Compare what you have with what others have.

5. Always be serious.

6. Take responsibility for everything all the time.

7. Try to please everybody all the time (never say "no").

8. Help others but don't let anyone help you.

9. Consider your own wants unimportant.

10. If anyone compliments you, discount it.

11. If anyone says anything, exaggerate it.

12. Always stay calm and cool.

13. Resist change to the death.

14. Strive for absolute perfection.

15. Always live in the past or in the future.

THAT FEELINGS OF USELESSNESS AND SELF-PITY WILL DISAPPEAR

1) It turns flaming idiots into balls of fire that go around lighting everyone's candle.

2) Stop trying; start working.

3) Being out of your mind is actually a good thing… it is far better than being in your mind.

4) Heal the heart and you heal the mind.

TECHNIQUES FOR THINKING

1) Keep life simple.

2) Practice being satisfied.

3) Beware of indecision.

4) Practice cheerfulness.

5) Learn to like people.

6) Live and Let Live.

7) Use adversity.

8) Don't take yourself so seriously.

9) Have a sense of humor.

10) Practice objectivity.

11) Tolerate your own mistakes.

12) Forgive yourself.

WE WILL LOSE INTEREST IN SELFISH THINGS AND GAIN INTEREST IN OUR FELLOWS

1. Real humility requires some to forgive themselves for the thought that they were better than others.

2. Growing by the inspiration of others does not require you to accept the actions of others that inspire you.

3. Being inspired by those you honor and respect is good; being inspired by those you do not honor and respect is better.

4. It makes no difference who inspires you, friend or foe; it just matters that you are inspired.

5. Tolerance without love is just tolerance. Tolerance with love is acceptance.

6. When you tolerate someone without love, they experience tolerance; when you tolerate someone with love they experience acceptance.

7. Before you strive to win the battle make sure it's the one you want to win.

8. In the program you find hearts healing hearts.

9. In the fellowship you discover it takes a heart to heal a heart.

10. The fellowship in action—hearts healing hearts.

11. He is a normal person in his own mind.

12. Hatred and resentment are the weeds in the garden of your mind while love and tolerance are the plants. Honesty and willingness are the fertilizers for your garden.

13. Three more important words in the program: humility, humility, and humility.

14. We come to the rooms feeling special, and then we become humble.

15. To really hunger is to begin to understand.

THE FIVE HINDRANCES TO GROWTH

1. Sense desire... future oriented.

2. Hatred; anger, ill will, annoyance, irritation.

3. Sloth/torpor/laziness... let me go to sleep.

4. Restlessness... jumping from one thing to the next.

5. Doubt (perhaps most difficult of all) doubt in oneself or what one has chosen to do... "I can't do it;" "why do I want to?"

SELF-SEEKING WILL SLIP AWAY

1) Spirituality requires some of us to give up food as our higher power.

2) 12-step meetings: where you get to meet yourself.

There is a power in our thoughts. We create our own surroundings by the thoughts we think. Physically, this may take a period of time, but spiritually it is instantaneous. If we understood the power of our thoughts, we would guard them more closely. If we understood the awesome power of our words, we would prefer silence to almost anything negative. In our thoughts and words we create our own weaknesses and our own strengths. Our limitations and joys begin in our hearts. We can always replace negative with positive.

Because our thoughts can affect this eternal energy, they are the source of creation. All creation begins in the mind. It must be thought first.

OUR WHOLE ATTITUDE AND OUTLOOK UPON LIFE WILL CHANGE

1) You are bribed with unbelievable promises that at first you do not believe.

2) Definition of insanity-- doing the same thing over and over, knowing you will get the same result and praying that it would be different.

3) Resentment is cancer of the mind. If you do not kill it, it will kill you.

4) A 12-stepper is a person who sees that life sucks and does something about it.

5) Old-timer—one who HALTED (happy, aligned, loving, tolerant, enlightened, and dependable).

6) The successful old-timer—a beginner with years under his belt.

7) Some people take steps; others do steps.

8) Bringing the little train that thought it could to life.

9) To the newcomer: after you have gone down the yellow brick road, you can take the road to recovery back home.

10) Working the steps is like kneading dough; if you keep doing it you will eventually rise.

11) The good news is that you can actually put a round peg in a square hole.

12) Life is not broken, nor needs to be fixed.

Our deepest fear is not that we are inadequate,
Our deepest fear is that we are powerful
Beyond measure.

It is our light, not our darkness, that most
Frightens us. We ask
Who am I to be brilliant,
Gorgeous, talented, fabulous?

Actually, who are you not to be?
You are a child of God.

Your playing small doesn't serve the world.
There's nothing enlightened about shrinking
So that other people
Won't feel insecure around you.

We are all meant to shine, as children do.

We were born to make manifest
The glory of God that is within us.

It's not just in some of us;
It's in everyone.

As we let our own light shine,
We give other people permission to do the same;

As we're liberated from our own fear,
Our presence automatically liberates others.

FEAR OF PEOPLE AND OF ECONOMIC INSECURITY WILL LEAVE US

1) The genuine baptism under fire.

2) Love and tolerate others as you love and tolerate yourself.

3) The program proves that love alone is not enough. You can love someone and not accept them; you can tolerate someone and not accept them, but you cannot love and tolerate someone and not accept them.

4) The 12-step program is where you are urged to be out of your mind.

5) Getting on your knees is encouraged to help you pray; getting up is encouraged to help you stay.

6) The fellowship: brotherly love healing hearts.

7) Do not be a turkey and be killed to make people happy.

8) Spiritual minds think alike.

9) Be like a babe and go listen to stories.

I am your constant companion. I am your greatest helper or heaviest burden. I will push you onward or drag you down to failure. I am completely at your command. Half the things you do you might just as well turn over to me, and I will be able to do them quickly, correctly.

I am easily managed—you must merely be firm with me. Show me exactly how you want something done, and after a few lessons I will do it automatically. I am the servant of all great people; and alas, of all failures as well. Those who are failures, I have made failures.

I am not a machine, though I work with all the precision of a machine plus the intelligence of a human being. You may run me for a profit or turn me for ruin—it makes no difference to me.

Take me, train me, be firm with me, and I will place the world at your feet. Be easy with me and I will destroy you.

Who am I?

I am habit.

-*Anonymous*

WE WILL INTUITIVELY KNOW HOW TO HANDLE SITUATIONS THAT USED TO BAFFLE US

1) The real winner focuses on the war and not the battle.

2) The program clears the dead trees in the forest so that you can see the trees that are trying to grow.

3) Let go of your thinking to find your right mind.

4) A beginner can get confused and try to take 12 steps instead of doing the 12 steps.

5) The mind is a good servant but a poor master.

6) Mastermind: making your mind your servant.

7) When your head is in the clouds it is hard to see the ground.

8) When your head is in the clouds you cannot see the path and you will get lost.

9) A miracle is an acknowledgement that an unexpected and good event occurred.

LETTER FROM A FRIEND

I just had to write to tell you how much I love you and care for you. Yesterday I saw you walking and laughing with your friends. I hoped that soon you'd want Me to walk along with you, too. So I painted you a sunset to close your day and whispered a cool breeze to refresh you. I waited—you never called—I just kept on loving you.

As I watched you fall asleep last night, I wanted so much to touch you. I spilled moonlight onto your face—trickling down your cheeks as so many tears have. You didn't think of me; I wanted so much to comfort you.

The next day I exploded a brilliant sunrise into a glorious morning for you. But you woke up late and rushed off to work—you didn't even notice. My sky became cloudy and my tears were the rain.

I love you, oh, if you'd only listen. I really love you. I try to say it in the quiet of the green meadows and in the blue sky. The wind whispers My love throughout the treetops and spills it into the vibrant colors of all the flowers. I shout it to you in the thunder of the great waterfalls and compose love songs for birds to sing for you. I warm you with the clothing of My sunshine and perfume the air with nature's sweet scent. My love for you is deeper than any ocean and greater than any need in your heart. If you'd only realize how I care.

My Dad sends His love. I want you to meet Him—He cares so. Fathers are just that way. So, please, call on me soon. No matter how long it takes, I'll wait, because I love you!

Your friend,

Jesus

WE WILL SUDDENLY REALIZE THAT GOD IS DOING FOR US WHAT WE COULD NOT DO FOR OURSELVES

1) The weaker you are the more you pick up; and the stronger you are the less you pick up.

2) Where the spiritual meets the physical and gets emotional.

3) Where the emotional meets the physical and gets spiritual.

4) The Old Testament, the Sermon on the Mount, how a man thinketh, and the greatest thing in the world—LOVE.

5) The new testament of the twelve steps—the big book.

6) The twelve traditions are the commandments of the program.

7) It is where you can see miracles—the ignorant become wise; the unhealthy become healthy; and the blind can see.

8) We are all born saints; a few of us remain that way.

9) Miracles happen for you when you believe.

10) The road to recovery requires you to cross the rivers of belief and willingness.

11) A spiritual awakening occurs when you stop shooting the messenger and receive the message.

12) It is far better to know God's will and tell him you are not yet ready than to keep asking him for His will and later saying, "I don't know."

13) If the kingdom of heaven is within, then God's home is in your heart.

14) The program teaches you to be a good soldier by following the commander.

15) The program takes you from know-it-all to one who knows that he does not know it all and is content with not knowing it all, and knowing who knows it all.

16) A philosophy in which one comes to the belief that he cannot live a good and decent life alone and that others can help him if he reaches out and that there is one ultimate authority.

What I do today is important because I am exchanging one day of my life for it.

Every morning you are handed 24 golden hours. They are one of the few things in this world that you get free of charge. If you had all the money in the world, you couldn't buy an extra hour. What will you do with the priceless treasure? Remember, you must use it, as it is given only once. Once wasted you cannot get it back.

SPONSOR/SPONSORSHIP

1) Changing sponsors at will is good as long as you do not use your will to change the message.

2) The reason for a sponsor is to avoid the phenomenon of the passing of messages. When more than one messenger is used to carry the message it gets distorted.

3) A sponsor is like a nutcracker. He wants to break open the shell without cracking the nut.

4) It is a verbal book club that listens to the same stories over and over again.

5) It is a program of reciprocal promises.

6) The question is, do you see it as a spiritual program of recovery, or is it a program of spiritual recovery?

7) Abstinence allows one to begin their emotional and spiritual recovery.

8) Making a decision is a good start; acting on it is success.

9) Taking what is said out of the rooms is a sin against the program.

10) An attitude of gratitude increases your altitude and enables you to soar above the turbulence of life.

11) When a compulsive eater is bingeing he has fear and he gets frozen in his tracks; when the compulsive eater gets abstinent he has the courage to stand on high ground.

SPONSOR

1. One who assumes responsibility for another person or a group during a period of instruction, apprenticeship, or probation.

Sponsor – someone who supports or champions something

Supporter, patron

Benefactor, helper – a person who helps people or institutions (especially with financial help)

Backer, angel – invests in a theatrical production

Godfather – someone having a relation analogous to that of a male sponsor to his godchild

Godparent – a person who sponsors someone (the godchild) at baptism

Guarantor, warranter, warrantor, surety – one who provides a warrant or guarantee to another

Patroness, patronne – a woman who is a patron or the wife of a patron

Pillar of strength, tower of strength – a person who can be relied on to give a great deal of support and comfort

SPONSOR/SPONSORSHIP-CONTINUED

12) It is important to grasp the point that he knows he's not all there; then he is able to grasp the will of God.

13) Just because you are moving, it does not mean you are taking the steps.

14) An INACTIVE compulsive eater is one who is active with the steps.

15) Making a decision in step three is a good start; acting on it is success.

16) One who has accepted his calling.

17) To give is more powerful than to receive.

18) Bill Wilson: an example of the power of giving over receiving.

19) The critical step is when a person takes to making amends.

20) A fellowship of believers who trust in God and believe they received a gift in order to give it away.

21) Let us not forget the real intent of a boomerang is to give you a second chance.

22) Think less; do more.

23) Sponsor: one who spoon feeds.

24) A sponsor is like a nutcracker- he wants to break open the shell without cracking the nut.

25) Sponsor- a peach.

26) Sponsor- a lime.

27) Sponsor- a prune.

28) Sponsor- your spiritual drill sergeant.

29) It does little good to get a sponsor if you turn a deaf ear.

Service to others is the crowning glory of one's being, the gift one is given to be of service to one who is suffering is a gift that never wears out, always stays fresh, can be taken in small bites, feeds others, and nurtures oneself. May I always look to be of service to my fellow human being who still suffers.

SPONSOR/SPONSORSHIP-CONTINUED

30) Sponsor- one who guides you through the jungle of life.

31) Sponsorship satisfies hunger for reciprocation by feeding others with program food.

THE PROBLEM WITH THE FOOD PYRAMID IS THAT IT DOES NOT GIVE GUIDELINES FOR THE TYPE AND QUANTITIES OF SPIRITUAL AND EMOTIONAL FOOD ONE MUST HAVE TO BE REALLY HEALTHY. SUGGESTION: HAVE 9 SERVINGS OF SPIRITUAL FOOD, 5 SERVINGS OF EMOTIONAL AND THREE MEALS A DAY OF FOOD FOR YOUR PHYSICAL BEING.

GRATITUDE

1) The program is where your grocery list is replaced with your gratitude list.

2) Life's lemons, although somewhat bitter, can be exactly what you must be fed.

3) Salvation: freedom from salivating.

4) Count your blessings instead of counting your calories.

5) Some people gain weight just looking at food and watching it disappear, and others lose weight by looking at the food, without it disappearing.

6) Abstinence comes one meal at a time.

The 12-step programs have delivered to millions and millions of people who could not help themselves, and who could not be helped by conventional means. It is alternative medicine for the mind and spirit. It has been said that the twelve steps are America's 20th-century spiritual contribution to the world. I personally was told to find an excuse to get into a twelve-step program and am very glad I did. May this book make a contribution to all who open it, for that is my mission.

Appreciatively,

Carlo John Palmieri

AKA *Tuchy*

Also by Tuchy Palmieri:

The Platinum Rule and Other Contrarian Sayings

(BookSurge, 2006)

Tuchy's Law And Other Contrarian Quotes to Help You In Life's

Journey

(BookSurge, 2007)

Off The Wall Contrarian Quotes For People In Recovery

(BookSurge, 2007)